A 20 Year Retrospective of Writers in Schools and an Anthology: 1982–1985

The Ohio Arts Council was established in 1965 by the Ohio General Assembly. The Council provides a wide variety of programs and services in the performing, visual, literary and design arts available to artists, community groups and organizations throughout the state.

For additional information about residencies write to:
Vonnie Sanford, Coordinator
Artists in Education Program
Ohio Arts Council
727 East Main Street
Columbus, Ohio, 43266-0540
Voice and TDD 614/466-2613

Edited by **Robert Fox**
Writer in Residence

Artists in Education Program/**Poetry and Creative Writing**

Ohio Arts Council
727 East Main Street
Columbus, Ohio 43266-0540
Voice and TDD 614/466-2613

Published by the Ohio Arts Council

Printed in the United States of America

All views expressed in the feature articles are the personal opinions of the authors and do not necessarily reflect the policies of the Ohio Arts Council, the National Endowment for the Arts or any other organization.

Front cover art and design by Joel Lipman
Additional cover art by Micheal Milligan
Book design by Micheal Milligan, Robert Fox and Kasey Jones

This anthology and the Artists in Education Program are partially supported by a grant from the National Endowment for the Arts, a federal agency in Washington, D.C.

Library of Congress Cataloging-in-Publication Data

Main entry under title:

The World is flippied and damzled about.

"Artists in Education Program/Poetry and Creative Writing."
Summary: A collection of essays about the origins of writers in schools and poems written by Ohio students.
1. English language—Composition and exercises—Study and teaching—United States—History—Addresses, essays, lectures. 2. Creative writing—Study and teaching—United States—History—Addresses, essays, lectures. 3. School verse—Ohio. 4. Children's writings, American—Ohio. [1. Creative writing. 2. Children's writings. 3. American poetry—Collections] I. Fox, Robert, 1943- . II. Ohio Arts Council.
PE1405.U6W67 1986 808'.042'071073 85-31969
ISBN 0-913335-03-7

Table of Contents

For schoolchildren everywhere
. . . especially my own Joshua and Jessica

Introductions

RICHARD F. CELESTE
GOVERNOR

STATE OF OHIO
OFFICE OF THE GOVERNOR
COLUMBUS 43266-0601

October 23, 1985

The nation's attention has been focused on the rights and privileges of a good education and the responsibility of adults to provide it. We have excellent schools in Ohio and because of such vital programs as Artists in Education, we produce well-rounded students.

I'm very proud of the Ohio Arts Council's AIE Program, which teaches the basic skill of communication and encourages creativity in our youths. These are the keys to a successful life. Through such programs, our schools will continue to produce leaders in the arts and all aspects of life.

This book proves we are succeeding in educating our youths and ourselves, and is also evidence of why the OAC's AIE Program is tops in the country.

Best regards,

Richard F. Celeste

Richard F. Celeste
Governor

From the Chair

You are about to embark on an adventure in literature which travels far beyond these printed pages. We began this journey 20 years ago when the Ohio Arts Council and National Endowment for the Arts were founded, and, fortunately, because of sincere support and significant funding, there is no end in sight. This book is a reminder of the sometimes rough, often rewarding path of the past two decades, and a celebration of the glories and trials of youth and the arts. Too, this volume stands as strong evidence of the value of our programs, a thorough education for our students and continued encouragement to make and keep the arts a part of all of our lives.

Jeffrey A. Cole
Chair, Ohio Arts Council

From the Director

The world may indeed be "flippied and damzled about," but I, for one, am thrilled that it is! Throughout the nation and state, there has been a wonderful turnabout in the arts, a "flip" towards making the arts accessible. The arts have been wrested from the grasp of an elitist reputation and placed into the hands of artists, encouraging them to create and make the arts accessible to all. Literature has been no exception.

The book in your hand is one small effort in spreading the good writing that we've had the freedom to sponsor and produce. It's a very large and very real effort to encourage continued creativity at the most basic level, in our schools.

The year 1985 itself has been a celebration of the wealth of artistic creations produced in the 20 years since the establishment of the Ohio Arts Council and the National Endowment for the Arts. We've taken time to examine our past efforts and improve on them. We continue to present our successes, such as the fifth in a series of anthologies produced through our Artists in Education Program.

This project is the result of a joint venture of many, many people. I offer my sincere thanks to Vonnie Sanford and Kay Allen, AIE coordinator and assistant coordinator, respectively; Council members who have strongly encouraged our outreach efforts in the schools; Governor Richard F. Celeste and the Ohio General Assembly, for supporting a sizable budget increase for the OAC; the NEA, for their continued support of our programs; Bob Fox, our writer in residence; Micheal Milligan, our graphic designer and design arts coordinator; and our support staff.

The World Is Flippied and Damzled About is a celebration of life and the freedom to publish—the result of a rewarding rapport among the OAC, the NEA, artists and students. Most notably, this volume is a celebration of the precious relationship between adult and child: An adult shares guidance and wisdom of ages and the child returns observations, though sometimes naive, wise beyond their years. *Enjoy!*

Wayne P. Lawson
Executive Director, Ohio Arts Council

From the AIE Coordinator

This volume, the fifth anthology produced through the Artists in Education Program, is dedicated to the 20th anniversaries of the Ohio Arts Council and the National Endowment for the Arts—20 years of support for the arts in Ohio, specifically through AIE, support for artists working in residency settings, each sharing his or her own vision and passion with residency participants.

It was with the writing component that this remarkable program began. In those early stages, as the feature articles document, a pilot program was funded at the national level to bring outstanding, established poets into schools for readings and discussion sessions with teachers to stimulate their interest in the art form. The program also included younger, lesser-known poets who read and discussed their own poetry with high school students. These efforts were located in six cities.

Response to the program was immediate. From those first activities in 1966, the program was formalized at the National Endowment for the Arts and other disciplines were gradually added. Today, artists in all disciplines are involved in residency activities in varied educational settings in all 50 states and the special jurisdictions. The program's strength is its reliance on the highest quality artists of professional excellence who also have unique and effective communication skills.

For the past several weeks, OAC's writer in residence, Bob Fox, has been unusually euphoric. The sounds emanating from Foxy's Corner (as his small office is affectionately known) have varied from humming affirmation to chuckles and finally, to loud, joyous guffaws. I know that it's Bob's favorite time of the year—the time that he spends immersed in reading and editing the children's poems, poems created over the past two years during residencies with many of

AIE's talented writers. The staff is regularly interrupted to hear yet another special poem.

We are all so very proud of this book. I offer my gratitude and sincere thanks to Bob Fox, who has, once again, surpassed his previous anthology; to Joel Lipman, who created such a wonderful cover; to the writers in this program; and to the hundreds of children who made this anthology possible. You all help to make my job the joy that it is! Ah, yes, the world is certainly "flippied and damzled about."

Vonnie Sanford
Artists in Education Coordinator, Ohio Arts Council

From the Editor

When I joined the Council staff as Poet in Residence in 1977, one of my first tasks as coordinator of the Poets in the Schools Program was to create what would become a series of paperback collections of work written by students in the residencies. Nine years later, I'm happy to present the fifth anthology in the series.

As I've edited each book from the dozens of residency "samplers," the book in process becomes my favorite. The work takes me straight to the core of the residencies themselves: the "genius" that lies dormant like Aladdin's genie in all schoolchildren. The explosive joy of self-discovery compares with few other human experiences.

Self-realization is unquantifiable. Like the gift of life itself, it is a brilliance impossible to describe in statistical terms. The numerous successes that come from the program are as varied as individual lives, but there are patterns: the "problem" students, usually kids from broken homes, who have little or no self-esteem and are given futures by an artist's visit; and the average and good students, whose interests are broadened, their imaginations enhanced, their scholastic achievement improved.

The student poems that follow are by no means the work of polished poets, but they are flashes of light from previously untapped sources. Though many of the pieces are first takes, occasionally there appears a work surprisingly sophisticated in technique, coming from an intuitive sense of language and metaphor. I have selected work that shows flashes of fresh vision, surprising energy, engaging wisdom or disarming candor. My only regret is not having the room to include more of the fine work coming from the residencies, but that would take a book two or three times this size.

Apart from the freshness of the students' work, this anthology celebrates the 20th year that poets and other creative writers have been entering our public and private elementary and high schools nationally. To mark the anniversary, I have prepared a book within a book by including a series of articles to document and commemorate the history and meaning of the program.

Elizabeth Kray describes the origin of the first pilot project in New York City in 1966. As executive director of the Academy of American Poets, she had taken on the brave work of opening doors and gathering the poets to enter them. Leonard Randolph, a poet himself, saw the value in the pilot readings program and recalls how he created the national program of residencies by poets, which later involved other artistic disciplines in the Artists in Education Program as we know it today. Daniel Lusk, who worked the upper Midwest and mountain states in the early years, gives us a lyrical account of his travels. My own piece connects the success and growth of writing residencies to the increasing appearance of small presses as they became the center of literary publishing. Ron Padgett candidly assesses the program's strengths and weaknesses and offers positive suggestions for the future.

In one sense, my own biography parallels the history of writers in the schools, for I had the good fortune to participate in the Academy's first pilot project in 1966 and have been involved in Ohio's program since 1974. The past 20 years, as both poet and administrator, have been a very special joy for me, which I hope these pages will impart to you. Please join me in wishing the program a happy 20th and many more years to come!

As always, the title of this year's anthology is taken from a student poem. See if you can locate it!

Special thanks to all who made this book possible: the contributors; OAC colleagues, especially Wayne Lawson, the best boss a poet could have; Vonnie Sanford and Kay Allen of the

AIE Program; Kasey Jones for editorial wisdom and proofreading; Micheal Milligan for additional cover design and visual wisdom; and Rosemary Applegate, for a mountain of typing from rough manuscripts.

Thanks are also due to the numerous parents, teachers, school administrators, Council members and legislators, who all have made and continue to make the program a reality. And thanks, too, to the National Endowment for the Arts, where it all began.

Robert Fox
Writer in Residence, Ohio Arts Council

THE WORLD
IS
FLIPPIED
AND
DAMZLED ABOUT

A 20 Year Retrospective of Writers in Schools

Poetry in the Schools: New York, 1966/*Elizabeth Kray*

In 1966—over a generation of poets ago—the first Poetry in the Schools program started up in New York City. The next year, honed into a model, it was exported to Detroit and Pittsburgh, and the following year to Minneapolis, Chicago, Tucson and Los Angeles, all according to a master plan. The master plan had evolved from terms of a grant (and subsequent booster grants) issued by the National Endowment for the Arts to the Academy of American Poets, of which I was then executive director. Since I had initiated the New York program, I was also responsible for getting it into these other school systems.

As originally designed, one-half of the project, an in-service course on poetry taught by eminent poets, was aimed at teachers; the other, classroom readings by young poets, at students. A pledge of $10,000 from the Rockefeller Foundation (due to the imaginative support of Gerald Freund, then a humanities officer) helped attract additional grants. Because our grant from the NEA called for extension beyond New York City to two other cities, I had chosen Pittsburgh and Detroit as good candidates, which indeed they turned out to be, able to sustain both the teachers' course and the school readings.

I was naive enough to think New York's Board of Education would welcome the offer of these twin programs, all expenses paid. Nowadays it is taken for granted that poetry, art, dance and music may be taught within the public educational system by the artists themselves, so it is hard to believe what vehement opposition we encountered. It seems absurd that the request for sponsorship of a course moderated by Stanley Kunitz with such guest lecturers as W.H. Auden, Robert Lowell, Denise Levertov, Allen Tate, Robert Penn Warren, *et al.*, should be flatly rejected by the in-service bureaucracy. Why this opposition? I doubt that it was little more than reflexive bureaucratic resistance to any idea extrinsic to departmental thinking. (How some clever, wise supporters took up the fight and won the board over makes a good story, the telling for elsewhere.) Once we were accepted, the board appointed Harold Zlotnik as liaison between the board and the Academy, an apt choice. Zlotnik, then a member of the Curriculum Revision Bureau, was a former English teacher and departmental chairman who wrote poetry.

The in-service course was launched at the beginning of spring term 1966, generating enthusiasm among attending English teachers. This may have helped ease the way for acceptance in principle of the classroom program. Zlotnik guided me throughout the process of implanting the poetry readings into the New York system. First we were to secure the backing of the Standing Committee of English Department Chairmen, an advisory body to the board with a rotating membership. Coming into their meeting was like entering the temperate zone, compared to the arctic of the board.

It was an all-male committee that semester, alive to poetry, full of wit and wry humor. You could see these men as bright kids who had prospered in the public schools, gone to City College, and then enamored of education, had circled back to secondary schools to teach.

After some sharp but good-natured quizzing, the committee unanimously endorsed the program and also corroborated the set of procedures Zlotnik had worked out and which we followed from then on.

1. On board stationery, Zlotnik informed each high school superintendent of the program's availability and the chairman's approval.
2. We followed up with a letter describing the program and an application which the English de-

partment chairman could return to us if he wished.

3. We then sent the name and a photograph of the poet chosen for the school and a brief, unpretentious *vita* engagingly written in the first person by the poet. If possible, we included a book jacket and some poems, all intended for the bulletin board.

We received 117 applications in the return mail. Our first wave of poets entered the schools in early March. Then their letters came flooding in. (I had asked each poet to write a personal account of his experience, telling whatever struck him as important, negative or positive, rather than give a standardized report.) We learned so much so fast that now it is difficult to remember our original expectations beyond the desire to introduce poetry to young people as a natural and desirable part of human expression. We believed the language of contemporary poetry would speak directly to them as would the voices of the young poets. We wanted to sweep away the idea that poems were artifacts made for textbook display. For all these reasons we had resisted advice to formulate a methodology. Everything was trial and error for the poets were breaking new ground. We had few instructions to give.

We collected a pool of young poets mainly through the help of Denise Levertov and Galway Kinnell, who themselves could qualify under that broad category of "young poet." Stanley Kunitz and other senior poets also made recommendations. We started with about 30 poets participating, which does not take into account out-of-towners, such as Adrienne Rich, John Haines and others who would give readings while in New York. The numbers increased dramatically in the following years. Among the young fry were Louise Gluck and June Jordan, and among the more established poets were

David Ignatow, Galway Kinnell, Edward Field and Diane Wakoski. It is impossible to name them all.

These letters that flooded in, the fresh, unhackneyed responses of that first year, elated and troubled us for with them came new problems, one succeeding another. The poets had touched a magic button; a lid had flown up letting loose concerns we had not anticipated but that suddenly lay at our door.

One must remember that in the 1950s and early 1960s, teacher training had excluded any study of contemporary poetry. Faithful to their training, English teachers usually taught poetry by putting primary emphasis on the study of form as if poems were mainly constructed for the sake of fulfilling intricate rules. This meant that the young poets—through the act of reading unrhymed, free verse and discussing it as authentic poetry—were undermining the conventional pedagogy. The differences in outlook between the poets and the teachers sometimes got worked out in productive interactions.

> *May 9, 1966, Flushing*
>
> . . . I was the main speaker at an English department meeting, my subject being (much to my surprise) "Methods of Teaching Poetry in New Ways." Ahem. Well, we had a most dynamic exchange, lots of disagreement. Some teachers on my side—my side being the thoughts I was having at the moment, based on my reading experiences this spring . . . others insisting that, for example, modern poetry was not as important to teach and rhymed poetry should be stressed in creative writing periods. Lots of arguing. And some very fruitful idea-results.
>
> *Kathleen Fraser*

Black poets reading to classes of Black students began to iron out discrepancies separating the academic image of poetry from their own ideas of what poetry might mean to a ghetto child. "I found the first task was to disarm the students of their notions of poetry. Ghetto children, because the only contact they have with poetry is that of correct, dull, 19th century gentlemen (poets) . . . seem to feel that poetry is 'sissy' or some kind of interesting valentine," wrote Ishmael Reed.

Black poets also found themselves trying to resolve the problems these children faced in their attempt to reconcile the language of the home and street with the language of books.

> *May 28, 1966 (Junior High)*
> I spoke to them first about English as a metaphorical language, explaining metaphor and giving examples that crop up in their everyday speech, like "It rained cats and dogs" . . . or borrowing from some of the so-called slang expressions of Harlem speech such as "selling the wolf tickets" or "getting somebody told." Interestingly enough every child, in all periods, was acquainted with these expressions which come from the underground and are rich in imagery.
>
> *Ishmael Reed*

I was reminded of Tolstoy's struggle in his peasant school to break through the students' indifference to the "language of books." Despite their lively intelligence, Tolstoy's little pupils could not grasp that formal language was not merely a dialect of the nobility, but an instrument that could bring them personally the grace of knowledge.

We maintained the New York program for a number of years, along with the addition of some offshoots it had generated: Saturday poetry workshops for high school students held in branch libraries (well attended) and programs for teachers. The classroom readings inspired the initiation of a poetry journal for high school teachers, edited by poet Bill de Voti, who was also a teacher. Kenneth Koch one day asked if he could tackle grade school children and we found him P.S. 61 with its obliging principal; the outcome was his demonstration of ways to stimulate children to write.

By this time, poetry readings in the schools had become acceptable, indeed welcome, and it was a pleasure to witness their proliferation in various parts of the country.

What gives me pleasure in retrospect are memories of the poets' reactions to the experience. That reading their own poems to the kids gave them a more acute perception of their writing was self-evident, but there was a deeper pull, the pull between poet and audience that reminded one of legendary times when hearing poems was a vital part of daily life.

> *May 28, 1966*
> These kids have no literary sophistication, no education or pretense, and are really terrific. Everything straight across the board. "Do you write those poems when they happen, right there or wait until you get home?" "Why do you stop after every word?" (This led into a beautiful discussion of prosody with questions and statements on both sides; the questioner looked like he ran whatever gang he ran with, that subtle air of authority, who didn't need it, if that's clear) . . . . Well, it was interesting for us all, I'd never been more clear and direct and it's a shame it wasn't taped, I'll never do it the same way again, it was for him . . . .
>
> I was leaving the place, finally. The rain had stopped, sun beginning to try. Outside the tower-

ing doors, I put down the bookbag, the umbrella I'd brought and the WELCOME PAUL BLACKBURN sign which I wanted to have and brought with me. Changing into dark glasses. Six guys playing a fast handball game in nearby court. 2:45 in the afternoon. One shouted in between points, "Hey! There's the poet. Hi!" I waved cheerfully. Bag was too damned heavy, and walked toward Pitkin Avenue.

Thanks for this, Betty, whatever the program gets to or doesn't it pays me love.

Paul Blackburn

Elizabeth Kray moved to New York City from the University of Washington in 1950 and almost immediately became involved in arts programs, first at the Institute of International Education, next as assistant to the director of the famed Poetry Center at the YMHA. In 1963, she became executive director of the Academy of American Poets, a post she held until 1981. Recently, she has been coordinating literary-historical walks based on the lives of Melville, Poe and Whitman in New York City.

Origins: A Reminiscence/*Leonard Randolph*

Early on the second morning of her term as the second chairman of the National Endowment for the Arts, Nancy Hanks called me on the phone and said, "Len, I've been looking over the programs again, and I'd like some ideas from you about what we can do for literature."

It was 6:15. And given the normal course of things in those days of under-staffing, I had been sleeping on the couch in the State and Community Programs office which I was assistant director of at that time.

The phone call was a good indicator of what things were going to be like during the early months of Miss Hanks' career with the Endowment. Indeed, those days were a fair barometer of the weather during her entire remarkable tenure with that agency.

Miss Hanks was a doer, a mover, a careful analyst, a stateswoman, a charming and often beguiling woman who was among the most politically shrewd persons I had ever encountered, in or out of government.

The memorandum I gave her within an hour after she got to the office served as the foundation for a stronger and more viable program in literature than we had had before. This was largely because, of all the Endowment programs, Literature had been the most inadequately funded due to a lack of strong voices in its support or a unified demand of any kind from its wide but fragmented constituency.

Although my primary responsibilities with the Endowment at that time lay in working with the new state arts agencies, Nancy Hanks knew me as a writer who had been struggling to create an interest in writers and writing at the state arts council level. She also knew the Literature Program had, by neglect or accident, become the focal point of a persistent effort to sabotage support for the Endowment. Already the most critically under-funded of the Endowment's malnourished programs, Literature was in trouble where it counted—on the political front, on Capitol Hill.

A congressman who hailed from Iowa, my native state, had been mightily offended by a short story which was due to appear in an anthology of the best work from the country's literary magazines. The story was, among other things, a singularly graphic description of female genitalia in a state of advanced, if somewhat sophomorically exalted, state of exercise.

The congressman was similarly distraught by the appearance of a seven-letter poem entitled "LIGHGHT," the sole text of which was a repetition of the title in lower-case letters. Efforts on my part to defend the latter as a near-perfect verbal depiction of refracted light did little to calm the misgivings of some of our friends on "the Hill." They were not even persuaded when I cited Archibald MacLeish's famous dictum, "A poem should not mean, but be."

Despite the flashier aspects of the political trouble, lack of funds was by far the more severe problem. At this point (1969), the Arts Endowment and its fellow agency, the National Endowment for the Humanities, were among the newest federal programs. They had been created in the emotional backwash caused by the assassination of President Kennedy, along with numerous other programs loosely identified as part of Lyndon Johnson's "Great Society."

The creation of the Endowments was a truly bipartisan effort. A few congressmen and senators whose names appeared on the final enabling legislation had been fighting valiantly (Rep. Claude Pepper, for instance, comes instantly to mind) for many years to create some kind of ongoing federal commitment to the arts and to humanistic studies.

Once the agencies had been created, however, the White House made little effort to add muscle to their frail bones through adequate funding or vocal support for their goals.

Lyndon Johnson—a proud man with clearly defined visions of his own place in history—was stupidly insulted by one of his inner clique who planned a spectacular artists' gala for the White House without consulting anyone at the Endowment (including its first chairman, veteran Broadway producer and Democratic party fund-raiser, Roger Stevens). Since this event was scheduled during a time of particularly strong opposition to President Johnson's Vietnam policies, it was predictable that some of the writers and other artists present would use the occasion as a means of letting the White House know, as directly as possible, exactly how they felt.

They did so, with varying degrees of effectiveness, and LBJ got the message: From that day onward, the arts became an anathema to LBJ. Federal involvement in the arts, at any rate, had always been tenuous and problematical. Who can forget that glorious day in the House committee room when one of the distinguished members demanded to know of Hallie Flanagan, the director of the Federal Theatre, whether "this fellow Christopher Marlowe" had ever been a Communist?

As a result of a lifetime interest in the ways in which politics and politicians affect the lives of Americans, I had a fairly keen understanding of what some congressmen or senators might do for us—or to us.

I have dwelled on this background only because it is important to understand the context into which Miss Hanks was moving in dealing with the problems of Literature as a program.

In my memo to her, I had tried, as positively as I could, to deal with what I felt the program had been able to do in the past with ridiculously limited funding. Under the guidance of Carolyn Kizer, the brilliant poet and translator who had been the first director of the program, I pointed out:

1. We had created a series of small "Discovery Awards" which called attention to the work of writers who were just beginning to appear in print.

2. We had initiated a series of "Recognition Awards" for writers whose work was widely acknowledged as the product of genius, but who had received little or no financial success. (This later got us in more hot water when John Berryman, upon being informed he had been awarded $10,000 from the NEA, responded, "I don't know who the ______ they are, but if they want to give me ten thousand bucks, I'll sure as hell take it.")

3. We had established the precedent that the Endowment could legally give some indirect aid to a very few established literary magazines through a separately set-up and funded organization created by the Endowment.

4. At some length, I described a very small pilot program funded through the Academy of American Poets which was placing published writers in schools in a half-dozen major cities.

Well over half of that memo to Miss Hanks elaborated on this last concept. It had been my feeling for some time that this kind of program could be of enormous benefit, not only to individual writers and to writing in general, but equally to state arts agencies' efforts to build support for their programs within their own regions.

Through my daily contacts with existing state councils, I had already begun to create small, new projects, again on a pilot basis, which were almost instantly proving their effectiveness. I saw such programs as a way of taking literature more directly and dramatically into the mainstream of American life—if writers chose to do that.

My arguments in favor of a Poetry in the Schools program were essentially these:

1. It would provide, for the first time, areas of real employment for writers—primarily poets, but including fiction writers, playwrights and others—who would be paid decent amounts of money to take their work and go into a classroom, *as writers*, identifying themselves proudly and unabashedly as such *within their own communities*!

2. It would give the fledgling state arts agencies an opportunity to do something for writers and for writing, many of them for the first time.

3. With luck, it could give at least a small part of a whole generation a new idea of what poetry really is—a knowledge which could affect their attitudes toward writing and reading throughout the rest of their lives.

4. Finally, but certainly not least of all, it could create a whole new working relationship between the individual arts agencies in the field and the National Endowment—a relationship which, at that point, was in disrepair.

Underlying all of this was my abiding conviction that the program held the promise of creating a new attitude about teaching language to children. It was a way of making them see that their language *belonged to them*, that it was not something dry or dull or meaningless which existed only on a printed page, and *that they could use those words to express their own feelings, their fears, their own stories and, eventually, their aspirations.*

To illustrate the fight for recognition of literature *as an art form* within the Endowment, I recall one session of the National Council on the Arts, the superstar advisory body set up to lend its guidance and expertise to the Endowment's grants-making processes. A long, and for me at least, very painful discussion ensued when one of the artists on the Council asked, in all seriousness, "Tell me, why is there a Literature Program in the National Endowment for the Arts? Shouldn't that be in the Humanities?"

My reasons for going into such detail on the first point in my memo should be obvious to anyone who has considered him or herself to be a serious writer, particularly in a small community. When I was coming of age in the Bible Belt of the Midwest, the common question which nearly always followed the statement, "I'm a writer," was, "Oh, yes, but what do you do for a living?" Some things, I fear, do not change.

Miss Hanks' response to my memo was enthusiastic; she encouraged me to put together more precise plans. Meanwhile, she suggested we talk about poetry in the schools. As a result of that discussion, she verbally agreed to do everything in her power to somehow find a pocket of money which would enable us to expand the Poetry in the Schools Program and get it started as soon as possible in every state in the union. It took some doing, but three years later, she had lived up to that promise.

Nancy also asked me to become acting director of the Literature Program while still carrying on my duties in the states-related programs. I agreed. Less than a month later, after numerous attempts to find a successor for Carolyn Kizer as full-time director, Miss Hanks appointed me to the post. In doing so, she explained she wanted someone in the job who—although lacking the glamor of a well-known writer—would be strong and willing enough to fight for the recognition of literature as a vital, energizing force in the arts of our country.

In the following months, a good many state arts and education officials got to know the zeal I brought to the concept of the Poetry in the Schools Program. Much of the struggle centered around the selection of the writers, their primary role in the classroom and the desired result from having them there. Whereas the pilot program had concentrated on the novelty of having the writer in the classroom, live, reading from his or her own work, I felt the impact of the programs could be far greater. I clearly remembered the effect simply hearing T.S. Eliot read from the Quartets had had on me years before. But that occasion had come to me some years *after* I had decided to become a writer. Far more important to me was that extraordinary winter day in my first year in school when the teacher in that one-room school had read aloud to the class a small poem I had written the day before.

I wanted the poets to try, at least, to evoke a sense of creativity, a response in and from the students with whom they came in contact.

To some teachers—and to nearly all administrators and school board members—poetry was clearly supposed to rhyme; to be rigidly patterned in strong, precisely measured lines; and, most offensive of all, be pleasant or pretty.

Once the ground rules were suitably established, the facts show the program worked astonishingly well. As a matter of fact, on some occasions and for some administrators, it worked too well.

During the first couple of years, when more than 500 writers eventually began to take part in the program, I was constantly being called on to put out brush fires in various places around the country. Most of the conflagrations, not surprisingly, dealt with "dirty" words. It was a rare day in my office or on the road when I was not besieged by telephone calls from worried teachers, harried writers or frustrated administrators who, in turn, were being set upon by irate school board members. Almost without exception, I found any conflict could be resolved through patience and common sense. One particularly memorable confrontation came about when a 10th grade student in a rural area wrote a poem containing a couple of graphic terms normally associated with urban graffiti. When I finally tracked down the school board member who had been most disturbed by this sinful wordplay, I found I was calling a pay phone in the reception area of one of the few legalized whorehouses in America.

In most of my conversations and more formal meetings

with school board members, I generally found I could make the case for the program's validity by simply emphasizing that it was, in the truest sense of the term, a return to the basic concepts of education—readin' and writin', two of the three "R's" nostalgia had taught us to turn into icons.

There were many storm signals in those early days, but most of them were false, growing out of a lingering fear of *words* and a mistrust of *language*.

When, after a year or so, the results of the students' own work began to appear in print, the fight became less difficult. Residency anthologies possessed enormously persuasive quality. Many of them were cheaply made mimeos or photocopies since there was virtually no money in the program at that point for reproduction of work. But the sight of those slim volumes made the politicians on the Hill—and, to my further delight—the members of the National Council on the Arts, begin to pay serious attention when I talked about literature. The books also demonstrated how, given the proper tools and right incentives, even children considered uneducable by the system could be brought to a level of self-worth and self-evaluation that would enable them to write openly and very movingly about themselves and their lives.

Anthologies were not always consistent. There was an occasional eruption of "pretty" poems. One state anthology, for instance, was given over entirely to poems about bunnies with fluffy tails and pink noses all atwitch. Nowhere did the volume give the slightest indication these students were living and writing in the center of one of the nation's most beautiful and historic territories.

Nearly every anthology that came across my desk or was handed to me in multiple copies when I was out in the field had a strong and dynamic sense of place; most of the writers were real young human beings attempting to deal with the circumstances of an often tumultuous and troublesome world.

Most of it may not have qualified as poetry in the strictest academic sense of that word, but for me at least, it was an extraordinary celebration of the creativity of the human spirit.

When the time came to present the case for Poetry in the Schools to the National Council on the Arts, I made certain every Council member had copies of the best anthologies coming out of the program. The effect was remarkable; the impact on the Council's thinking was exhilarating. Both Miss Hanks and I were amazed and delighted at the number of Council members–opera stars, violinists, architects, conductors and actors–who joined the two recognized writers on the Council in urging that the program not only be funded at the level I had asked, but further, to find a way to allocate additional funds in the future.

The program's success was not limited to our dealings with the National Council, whose members might have been expected to appreciate the stirrings of creativity in the young. Members of Congress had begun to pay attention largely because their legislative and administrative assistants, many of them aspiring writers, had made certain their bosses not only saw the anthologies from their own areas, but also read them. Best of all, congressmen wrote or called Miss Hanks to say how impressed they were by the work they had seen. One sure sign of the program's impact on the Hill came in the daily requests I received for additional copies of the individual anthologies. We filled the requests instantly even though it usually meant I had to hand-deliver the books to the offices on the Hill, making sure that the proper assistants got them personally. It was time-consuming and often difficult, but in the long run, it paid handsome dividends not only for Poetry in the Schools, but for the Endowment as a whole.

The next time we went up on the Hill for reauthorization hearings, I made sure every committee member had access to anthologies from his or her district. At one point during the initial hearing, Miss Hanks leaned back in her chair and asked, "What are they all reading up there?" She chuckled with appreciation when I said, "Poems. From the kids back home."

The Endowment sailed through those reauthorization hearings (the process which keeps an agency alive, legally) and the appropriations process (which gives the agency the blood and nourishment to stay alive and flourish). The administrative and public relations skills of Miss Hanks and her deputy, Michael Straight, were never more evident than they were in those weeks. Their skills were greatly augmented by the tangible evidence congressmen and senators had before them of the kinds of work being done, every day, in their own backyards.

On the home front, some of the initial bugs in the programs were being removed. The state arts agencies were becoming more visible and able to prove their effectiveness; many of them were receiving, for the first time, substantial funding from their governors' budgets and far greater support in the halls of the state legislatures. One after another, the success stories began to come in: Wyoming was in the process of hiring a full-time coordinator; South Carolina, North Carolina, North and South Dakota, Minnesota, Ohio, Missouri, Maryland—the list grew with each passing day as states found funds to match increasing amounts for the program the following year.

There were also indications that a number of states were moving toward longer-term residencies when specific school districts indicated such an interest. And there were prospects for greater regional planning which could eventually provide more days and weeks of employment for an increasing number of writers each year. Most important of all the news: The program would reach into school districts in every mainland state and in both Alaska and Hawaii that next year.

In general, the outlook was excellent: All we needed was

to find more money and the program could conceivably go right on expanding. That money was available from Title III of the Education Act, which was, in theory, supposed to encourage, augment and promote programs in the arts. There was quite a bit of money in Title III—more, at that point, than in the Endowment's entire budget.

The prospect of getting a cut of that pie was alluring to Miss Hanks. She was under enormous pressure to put ever-larger sums into existing arts institutions and there was, quite simply, not enough money to go around. Miss Hanks saw the possibility of using Title III funds to radically increase appropriations for putting writers in schools without putting a further dent in the Endowment's own meager funding, and, in response to growing pressures from the states and moderate encouragement from other Endowment programs, to create new projects which would place all kinds of artists in school situations. Thus, the Artists in the Schools Program was born.

During the period when the new program was formed, Nancy made it clear I was to remain the Endowment coordinator for programs placing writers in the schools, a job I continued to fill until I left the Endowment.

Indeed, the strength of the programs involving writers had been so solidly established and the results of their work were so demonstrable that nothing short of total abolition of the program could have destroyed those projects. Nevertheless, as the Artists in Schools (or AIS) Program proliferated, it became evident some of the local sponsoring organizations were emphasizing portions of the program which lent themselves most easily to photo opportunities and the writers' recognition was being diminished.

Still, when the chips were down and the state agencies or local schools needed to have visible evidence (other than photographs) that the funds spent on such programs was a wise investment, not a frill, it was the students' writing that seemed to offer the most credible argument in their favor. The files in my office continued to bulge to explosive levels with reports from nearly all of the states, along with testimonial letters from writers, teachers and administrators who saw the real value of having a writer in their schools.

When I left the Endowment after 15 years, I was able to look back on a number of accomplishments in which I felt I could take some degree of personal pride or a sense of satisfaction.

In the Literature Program, we had been able to start and strengthen programs which gave no-strings-attached fellowships to talented creative writers; we had started funding programs for small, independent publishers which then published (and continue to publish) nearly all of the beginning writers who see print initially; we had set up a sometimes stormy, but generally effective system for providing grants to literary magazines; we had produced an admirable, if totally incomplete, series of public television programs on "The Writer in America," and no less than a dozen other programs or projects, including writers' residencies in a remarkable spectrum of environments. The worth of those programs can best be judged, perhaps, by the fact that they remain in effect to this time as major parts of the Endowment's Literature Program with very little change.

Yet, of all those programs, none gave me a greater feeling of personal achievement—or, to use an old-fashioned and unfashionable word, joy—than Poetry in the Schools. In this case, as in almost no other, I was able to say that we had done, efficiently and effectively, what we set out to do:

- Large numbers of writers—many of them still at a formative stage in their careers—had been given some degree of employment within their own states and their own communities.

- They were being recognized, while they were in classrooms, as *writers*.

- A great number of students had not only been exposed to the work of fine writers, but had also been convinced that they, too, could use *their* language to express their own feelings and observations and aspirations.

- A remarkable number of teachers had been stimulated and encouraged to do writing on their own and to approach the multiple frustrations of their teaching load with a fresh viewpoint and new vision.

- An equally sizable number of administrators had been able to qualify, quantify and justify the expenditure of funds for the arts in education, if they cared to do so.

- And an amazing number of poets and fiction writers had found that in addressing themselves directly to their "audience," they had been able to gain new and often highly constructive insights into their own work and the process of writing.

At this stage of the game, some of these points may not seem terribly impressive to the casual observer–some not even to writers who are just now beginning to participate in the program. But to those first writers who went into the classrooms–remembering all the problems those visits raised for them and for the teachers–the meaning of the program should be as great as it is for me.

The love and respect I felt for them was the fire that kept

me going through all of my days with the bureaucracy. These words are, quite simply, a salute and a tribute to all of those individuals—the writers, the teachers and administrators and the students—who made it work.

I am grateful. And anyone who has been touched, however remotely, by this program ought to be, too.

Leonard Randolph was director of the Literature Program at the National Endowment for the Arts and national coordinator of Poetry in the Schools during its advent and for the first few years of its existence. He is the author of two poetry collections, *Scar Tissue* (Hollow Spring Press) and *Wind Over Ashes* (Carolina Wren Press).

Photo by C. Gregorie

Poets in the Schools: A Retrospective/*Daniel Lusk*

Some of us buy a new notebook and a pencil box at the first hint of fall; I wash my car. There was a time I did little else but drive from town to town, writing at my old typewriter wherever I put it down and visiting schools to parent the writing of children. In those days I don't think I even bothered to unpack my canvas suitcase, except maybe to do laundry or to hunt for the mate to a sock.

A couple of months ago when I sold my dogeared car, it showed nearly 200,000 miles, nearly all of them logged since 1971 when I began to be a poet in the schools. Cleaning up the car to sell, I found–besides a few hairs of my old Scotty dog, MacDuff, still embedded in the fabric seats–it still carried a wonderful cargo of memories of people and places I have come to know while searching countryside and towns for the bright phrases and fresh imaginings of young and waiting poets.

Full of miles and poem fragments as it was, that car should be in the PITS (Poets in the Schools) hall of fame. For that matter, MacDuff should be there, too. Long since gone now, he led me down back streets and across neighborhoods I would not otherwise have seen in the dawn light as he went with me through the mountain west and middle west.

I've been told I was one of the first poets–before there was a national program–to go into the schools to urge youngsters to write seriously. And I recall the first session, the morning in South Dakota, that began my pilgrimage.

A teacher named Ann Miner in a country elementary school at Hermosa turned her class over to me. We cleared away the stiff desks (those days I thought it would make it *seem* like something new was going on) and sat in pairs on the hardwood floor. Each of us would study our partner until it came to us just what it was that made that other person uniquely her or him.

After a long silence nicked here and there by snickering, a confidential whisper was heard: "You need to blow your nose."

While I was not cured that day of my seriousness, I never took us all completely seriously after that. I was a traveling minstrel, a medicine show, a lecturer and fool.

The years filled up with ache and triumph as the roads stretched out and the trees MacDuff confided in grew further and further apart. And when MacDuff died, I took a pair of zebra finches for traveling companions, carrying them in and out of hotel rooms in a bamboo cage.

The places I have slept in 14 years arrange themselves in my mind like pictures in an exhibition: the sofas and floors and hearths of friends, the fold-out hide-a-beds and spare rooms, the rooms decorated with religious icons, stuffed animals and computer games. The white room of the hotel in Chamberlain, South Dakota, simple and stark as a country Baptist church. The uptown motel with "magic fingers" in the king-size bed and glitter on the ceiling. The pup tent in a friend's farmyard where I was waked early by the frantic cry of a peacock inches from my head.

The worst was probably the motel where, after paying my bill in advance through the bulletproof cashier's window, I spent the week in a bile-green room, hearing the intimacies of hourly trysts coming and going next door.

The towns I have visited bear names like Belle Fourche and Corsica, Lead and Spearfish, Newcastle, Gillette, Crow Agency, Horseheads, Great Neck, Lewes and Seaford. And I have migrated like a lost goose from one to the other in no particular order across South Dakota, Wyoming, Montana, New York and Long Island, south into Delaware and back again.

Despite the natural haze of recall, certain things stay vivid and fresh even after years have passed. I recall the rainy night I left a lonely highway somewhere on the Standing

Rock Reservation, following my car lights down the long, muddy and precarious road that carried me like a calf in a branding chute down into Bullhead, South Dakota. The town lay on a curve of the Grand River like a sliver of soap in a wash basin. Water was everywhere. It promised to be, and should have been, a terrible week. Monday morning the rain continued and the children waded waist-deep to the school.

That week a dozen years ago has telescoped into a soup of scraps, somewhat because I went back to Bullhead other times. The nearest telephone was 35 miles away in McIntosh. There is "no alcohol" on the reservation, yet the alcoholism rate was above 90 percent. It seemed to me the town was barely alive.

I especially remember two little girls who told me of seeing a ghost, the brand new legend of a flying saucer, and two boys in the fourth grade, Harold and James.

Harold and James were both new in town–one lived with foster parents, the other with a grandmother–and they fought continually to gain a place in the pecking order. They fought with each other mostly, a wrestling match whenever there was a lull in our goings-on. And they wrote nothing in our sessions.

Finally, on the last day of that first week there, I managed to convince each to write something. For James, the quiet one, it was a gem of personal introspection, three lines about his house (which was not *his* house), his room and "the gray suitcase under the bed." For Harold, it was a laser of cosmic bravado. He wrote:

> If I were the world
> I would shake James off.

Both boys must be in their early 20s by now. Many of the children I have knelt beside, cheering and coaching, now are grown, perhaps with children of their own. I wonder about them, the way an uncle thinks about his favorite nephews and nieces–where they are, who they have become and of course, whether they read poetry.

One young man–I met him during a week completely removed, at a workshop in a state training school for young offenders–called me years later to tell me he had just been married and his new wife wrote poetry. He knew I would be pleased. Thinking of him now I am reminded of the hours I had to write while I was there, hours secluded in a monk-like room, composing poems for my students, filling them with stories they would give me from their lives: of running away, of thievery, and the intimate mayhem they had been either guilty of or victims of. Secrets.

Half a state away at a school for the deaf, everything anyone said seemed somehow secret. Even the phrases they taught me to sign–I am a poet; I am hungry; I love you–seemed as if I'd never said or written them before. A senior boy (whose sport was bull riding) wrote this poem:

Voiceless hands always moving
Like you are pianoing.
Silent code
Like the Morse Code.
Voiceless mouth always closing
Like the zipper.

Mike Crago

These young people taught me, as young poets everywhere have taught me. And in my turn I brought them what I had: love of words, curiosity about their lives and a book-bag filled with the works of other living poets, the best I know about. I brought them surprises and beauty and horror and wisdom as true as I have learned to recognize it.

I gave them old friends of mine who write in relative obscurity: Robert Dyer, his simple and meditative book *Oracle of the Turtle* (Singing Wind); Patrick Todd, his *Fire in the Bushes* (Clearwater), both poets I have lost touch with but whose books I carry everywhere. Mark Vinz. Charles Levendosky.

And famous poets, who have taught me to write, to see, perhaps to teach: Galway Kinnell, Gerald Stern, Philip Levine, Ted Kooser, Stephen Dunn, Gary Gildner, William Stafford, Harley Elliott, all alive.

My favorite exercises for the children come one way or another from these and from a hundred other poets I read and carry with me. With the very youngest poets I have sometimes played "radio": They close their eyes and then I read to them a poem ripe with imagery.

Once after such a reading of a poem by Wendell Berry to a rapt workshop of six-year-olds, when I asked them to recall one word they liked especially in the poem, the group collectively gave me back the nouns and adjectives and verbs of almost the entire poem. And I wrote them down on the blackboard, word after thrilling word, and then asked them to pick out three or four they liked to make a poem. Here are some:

light	stone	rocks
star	star	mountain
bright	valley	star
sky	grass	sky

When I played radio with the second graders, I asked them to wait as they listened until they began to see in their minds the pictures the words made, and then to write a poem from their pictures:

I saw the trees singing
and. Swaying and. The
ground lifting up and.
I saw lights and. Saw
the tree whistling music.

Kurt Hussong

Nov. Friday dark of the sea
deep. Feeling something in him I know.
Rocks broken and shells broken
Glowing in the dark I heard the
world coming up I saw it
too. I like seeing it in mind.

Mandy Hoopes

None of the exercises I have tried are meant for a particular age group or grade level. I do the simplest things with the most intellectual students to get them to write concretely. And just as I try to read to students the best poems I know of (rather than those "children's poems" that are so trite they set your teeth on edge), I don't expect young writers will write "kid" poetry. Here is one by a fifth grader:

The Howling of the Bones

Walking in the forest, you see a
  wolf howling to the moon,
Your footprint filling the water.
You look up in the sky,
You see an owl howling, flapping
  his wings and winking his eye.
You see a camp fire that was never
  there.
You go to sleep without knowing it.
You're sleeping on raw bones.

Johnny Tucker

(Note the sophisticated use of several poetic devices.) Or this one by an urban fourth grader:

Dreams

I see a man in a white car move like
  a ghost on the skyline.
Take all your dreams and you throw
  them away,
  man in a white car.

Stephen Prosceno

I have loved the difficult students for the miracles of their poems. I recall a bully of an eighth grader who amazed himself and everyone else with the discovery of a talent for words and an incredible lode of gentleness. One of several fine poems:

The Perfect Poem

The perfect poem is about summer.
It is the summer of everyone's joy.
A summer of peace and plentiful food.
A summer when all people profit.
A sound of young children of all kind
crying out in happiness.

Jeff LaGasse

Once, a taciturn girl who at first refused to write made at last a pact with me. "You tell me what you are thinking," she demanded, "and then I will tell you." I wrote her a little poem. And later she brought me a note. It said, "I was thinking about my boyfriend and about wild horses."

And then there was the class clown and chronic troublemaker who found that if he wrote the best poems, he got lots of attention. I recall his innocence of the meanings of elegant words did not inhibit his elegant use of them.

A Made-up World

I'm conducting the stars and the
bright, bright sun. The moon
is in an orbit of charity. The
stars in space are virtually
beautiful.

Dameion Green
Grade 4

Actually, the young poets who had most difficulty with traditional English and grammar often produced the most exciting poetry, those writers for whom English was a second language, for example, the Crow Indian children in eastern Montana. Their native tongue had no words for abstractions, so their poems were never vague.

Dear Grass

I give you shadows, bats and moths
dogs barking and crying like the wind
blowing, or a man crying over love

sincerely

moon

Tom LaForge

Over the years, I have become accustomed to seeing teenage girls cry at the pain of some memory, or seven-year-olds cry with frustration or anxiety. I have learned that not being looked in the eye is a sign of respect in some places, that kneeling to talk with small poets can help some to write far over their heads.

I guess I have worked with over 10,000 young poets—with names like Yellow Earrings, Sharbono, Goes Ahead, May Morning, names like White, Higgins, Badger and Stone, like Chang, Miller, Jackson and Green, Duffield, Campo and Schwartz. And the one thing we all seemed to have in common is the feeling that where we live is no place special. That some other place is exotic enough for poetry, interesting enough to write about, but not here. That our lives are plain and embarrassingly dull, hardly the stuff of which literature can be made.

So the horseshoe crabs thrown up by the thousands onto the beaches around Lewes, Delaware. And the men in the schoolyards of Pine Ridge or Bullhead dancing the old dances, their American Legion uniforms adorned with feather bustles and ankle bells, feathers in their caps. So the yearling calf found in a farmyard outside Arlee, Montana, its shoulder torn away by a hungry grizzly bear. So the wounded buck deer following the railroad track into south Sioux Falls, crashing into the plate glass window of an auto parts store. So the great gaze of a moose in Glacier Park. Or the hundred treeless acres of trailer houses, like a lake of broken glass, outside Gillette, Wyoming. All ordinary, daily and normal to those of us who live with them, go home to them, wake up to them, week after week. The stuff of our lives is the stuff of our poems.

These years as traveling poet have been good because of the good teachers, and the optimistic administrators, and of course the brave children. And I would not dare to begin to thank the people I can sometimes only remember by the rug in their front hall, or the smell of their kitchen, the paperweight on their school desk or the freshness of their towels.

But I am especially indebted to Joe Fitzpatrick, to Leonard Randolph, to Dennis Holub, to Charles Levendosky and to Myra Klahr, some of whom are no longer where I met them, but who put me on wheels, and whose faith and help kept me going.

Not that all has been rosy. There have been the nasty school politics, sometimes the locals' natural distrust of strangers, the hostility of some teachers who feel threatened by a "visiting fireman," especially a younger one, and in some places, an icy snobbery to balance the love I found in others. And having been a classroom teacher it is hard to find fault with teachers who flee the room when the poet enters, as if he or she were a god-sent substitute and the key to an extra coffee break or planning period.

I have so many favorites among the thousands of poems I have been witness to that it is hard to pick one as being best, but there is a little group poem done by first graders in a Friends school. I was their secretary.

Worries

I worry about a dream I have.
I worry about gravity.
When I go to brush my teeth
I sing so no one will get me.
I worry about gorillas.
About getting hit by cars.
About my dog, that he'll get hurt.
I think monsters are under my bed.
I worry about my cat at the S.P.C.A.
I worry about my little brother because
he runs out in the street.

I worry about the alphabet because you never
know what it's going to say.

It's like that, too, with poetry.

Daniel Lusk is a poet, novelist and free-lance journalist who lives in eastern Pennsylvania with his wife and stepson. His books include *O, Rosie*, a novel (Carpenter Press, 1979); *Doors: Poems* (Red Dust, 1982); *Wild Onions*, poems (Bookmark, 1975); and *Homemade Poems: A Handbook* (Lame Johnny Press, 1974). A native midwesterner, he has worked extensively in the Poets in the Schools programs of South Dakota, Wyoming, Montana, New York and currently Delaware.

Writers in the Schools and a Revolution in Literary Publishing: Two Aspects of the Literary Revival*

/Robert Fox

Introduction

Serious writing in this country is experiencing an exciting revival. In one arena, every state in the country and the territories has an Artists in Education Program that places creative writers (as well as other artists) into elementary and secondary schools for residencies. The residency programs have effected a dramatic change in the way the "basics" of reading and writing are taught in many schools. In another arena, contemporary publishing is undergoing revolutionary change: the widespread publication of serious poetry and fiction by small, independent presses after the genres had been virtually abandoned by commercial publishers. Literary publishing is no longer dominated by a hierarchy of big businesses, but by a pluralistic group of small craftspeople scattered across the country. Residency programs came into being at the same time the independent press began to grow rapidly, in the mid-1960s. Both fed each other without a deliberate connection, and both continue to create a growing change in the public awareness of literature and the people who write and publish it.

My own career as a writer, poet in the schools, book publisher and arts administrator over the past 20 years has led me into both arenas of the literary revival; it has been only during the last few years that I have begun to view my various experiences as a cohesive whole. Without a career plan as

*This article appeared in slightly different form in a special artists in education issue of *English in Texas*, Volume 16, Number 3, 1985, published at the University of Texas at San Antonio. The author is grateful to the editors for permission to reprint.

such, I've become a fully involved participant in the most exciting literary period since the time of Marlowe and Shakespeare. I'd like to share some facts and observations about contemporary publishing, and some of my personal experiences in the classroom, all of which help explain a new acceptance and interest in poetry and fiction, writing and books.

I. Poets in the Schools to Artists in Education

By the early 1960s, poetry was probably the most misunderstood and maligned art discipline in this country. The only good poets were dead ones. Living poets were sissies. Ernie Kovacs' character Percy Dovetonsils simply affirmed a popular stereotype. As a more or less typical teenager growing up in the 1950s, sporting a flattop hairstyle and a passion for baseball, I accepted the stereotype, not having known any real poets. I had written poetry regularly until the sixth grade. I recall an unfinished portrait of Henry Wadsworth Longfellow moldering on the classroom wall—an apt symbol of my stifled interest and lack of success memorizing "Hiawatha."

During my senior year in high school in 1960, a well-meaning teacher attempted to prepare my honors English class for college by teaching us the New Critics' approach to text. The year before I had shocked an English teacher by protesting that Whitman's "I Hear America Singing" bore as much relation to real life as a love affair between Fred Astaire and Ginger Rogers. Now, as a senior struggling with textual analysis, poetry seemed more akin to the analytic sciences than to experience. Reading poetry was obviously not something one did for pleasure or enlightenment, any more than one would *play* with advanced calculus.

I was an unknowing schizophrenic, for I wanted to be a fiction writer, telling the truth about how people lived, loved and died. Poetry bore no relation to prose, in my view. Poetry was something useless and decorative, probably invented by the French and recited by people with phony British accents.

My feelings did an abrupt about-face several years after high school (but not in college) while chancing upon recordings of Dylan Thomas reading his own work. Suddenly I became aware of language as a form of music and immersed myself in the work of Shakespeare, Keats, Coleridge, Tennyson, Swinburne and Hopkins. I wrote poems again for the first time since puberty, exercises in off-rhyme, assonance and alliteration, and I finally understood the musical values of language that made for good prose.

I received my first publications then, in mimeographed or cheaply offset magazines in Miami and Peoria, surprising locations of literary activity. By chance, I applied to the High School Reading Program sponsored by the Academy of American Poets and the New York City Board of Education. I was accepted and found myself a junior member of a gang of 150 or so published poets infiltrating high schools in the five boroughs.

I read and talked about my own work and read a few pieces by others such as Sylvia Plath and Yevtushenko, and fielded questions from the students. At one school I was an instant celebrity. "He has a novel at Farrar, Strauss," one of my host teachers proclaimed to a colleague after I had simply explained I had forwarded the publisher an unsolicited manuscript. At a wealthy suburban school, a "sophisticated" junior wanted to know how poets were different from human beings.

Such programs presented a startling alternative to popular conceptions, for the living poet, clearly identified as a person rather than a creature (in most cases) entered the schools. Poets were suddenly valued, regarded as role models, and were certainly paid well for their services. The $100 a day fee was more of a reward for a long, hard apprenticeship (as in the medical and legal professions) than a fee for actual services.

Despite the celebrity status, a number of poets felt skeptical about the impact of the program and a few, like Kenneth Koch,[1] entered the classroom itself rather than the library, and engaged whole classes rather than select groups, in the process of writing. The impact was immediate and obvious. Students discovered that writing, usually a dread chore that caused suffering, could actually be fun—that they had active, creative imaginations, feelings that were valid and worth sharing, and that it was fun to play a match-up game with words, ideas and emotions.

Len Randolph has already documented how the national program was created and grew. Artists in Education is now run primarily with Endowment money; in some states, federal grants are generously matched by state subsidies. AIE provides funds for short- and long-term residencies by individuals and by companies (in theatre and dance). The demand for the program is so great today that many states can fulfill only about half the residency requests they receive each year.

Just as a "scientific" approach to text removed the connection between poetry and life, commercial publishing, taken over by the entertainment conglomerates, created the illusion that the novel and short story had joined poetry in obscurity and irrelevance. Small, independent presses, however, proved that fiction and poetry are indeed vital means of communication; similarly, AIE programs have proved that creative writing can be a form of entertainment and have offered refreshing alternatives to the orthodoxies of teaching English. Exercises created by writers have become so widely accepted that a new school of pedagogy has arisen, a result of a dialogue that takes place between teachers and writers.[2]

Many teachers have learned about alternative publishing from resident writers. Many writers who work in the schools publish widely in the small press; some are publishers themselves. Writers often bring their own books and books by friends or favorite contemporaries, books published by curious-named presses all across the country. In addition to books, classroom materials sometimes include broadsides, postcards, visual poems, cassette tapes, videotapes and films.

II. The Survival of Contemporary Writing in the Independent Press

As a writer often exchanging manuscripts with friends, I was astonished to come across novels which surely should have been published commercially. They probably would have been, prior to the major change of commercial publishing from a private to a corporate business. The newly formed corporations were quickly consumed by multinational conglomerates, primarily those involved in the entertainment or media businesses. I was not fully aware of the changes when I founded Carpenter Press in 1973, but like many other writers, I founded the press to get a few of the available manuscripts into print.

An Authors Guild study published in 1978 estimated that in the previous 20 years, over 300 mergers had taken place in the publishing business.[3] The numbers have increased rapidly since then, for publishing offers a small profit margin, and publishers are constantly being shuffled from one multinational to another as they divest and procure various properties. They do not publish books for profit in themselves, but for potential subsidiary rights, sales and/or profits, e.g., Hollywood or TV movie rights, T-shirts, stuffed dolls, not to mention mass-market paperbacks.

Many of the companies commonly thought of as book publishers are no longer identified with serious literature. Editors have lost a great deal of prestige (they too shuffle from one house to another even more quickly than the houses themselves change hands), and writers are greatly demoralized.

Among the practices of publishers to go after big bucks are novelizations of movies and popular television shows. I was surprised when one day I discovered an "All in the Family" series of "novels" on a drugstore rack in rural southeastern Ohio. A new, mutant species of writers has emerged in the last decade that makes its living doing novelizations. (This species has evolved from earlier ones that did copycat versions of best sellers with similar titles, e.g., *The Andromeda Strain* becomes *The Andropeda Strain*.)

Publishers also choose subjects first and find authors later. John Jakes was selected by Fawcett to write the Bicentennial Series–it was not an idea he conceived. The idea for *Jaws* was determined by computer–Peter Benchley was chosen later.

As I mentioned earlier, the alternative press blossomed as the commercial marketplace for serious writers shrank. In fact, there is a proportional relationship between the growth of the independent publishers and the increasing number of mergers and takeovers. According to *Publishers Weekly*, the number of books published commercially in the United States grew from 13,000 in 1950 to over 40,000 in 1974,[4] a figure which remains true today. However, very few of the 40,000 books published annually by the trade are serious fiction or poetry. The 20th edition (1984-85) of the *International Directory of Little Magazines and Small Presses* lists over 2,500 domestic independent publishers, considerably more than the 10th annual edition, which listed just under 1,000. The most recent *Small Press Record of Books in Print, 13th edition, 1984*[5] lists over 18,000 books, pamphlets, broadsides, posters and poemcards–even more than what the trade press published in 1950.

Despite a growing sophistication about the nature of contemporary publishing, two commonly shared myths about the independent press still prevail. The first continues to maintain that commercial publishing houses exercise superior taste and judgment, making available the best of what is being written; and the second, which is a corollary of the first, suggests that, at the least, independent presses are a minor league farm system for commercial publishers, and at the worst, either vanity or subversive presses.

The history of modern publishing indicates that the majority of classic writers were either self-published initially or published by friends. A partial list of writers who published their own major work includes Pope, Blake, Burns, Irving, Whitman, Mark Twain and Upton Sinclair. Self or small press publication tends to be the rule throughout history and not the exception. Although this century has seen remarkable publishing by such people as Alfred Knopf and editor Maxwell Perkins of Scribners, commercial publishers have discovered or sponsored only about 20 percent of the writers in this country—small presses and magazines have sponsored the rest.[6]

An inadvertent censorship created by the economics of the marketplace has kept news of the literary publishing revival from the general reading public. Readers constitute a market as do other consumers and are susceptible to the review media. Unfortunately, review space is granted mostly to those presses who invest heavily in advertising. Independent press books are seldom reviewed in major media because the presses cannot afford the advertising space, and because literary books are not media events as are novels by Judith Krantz or Harold Robbins.

Recently, however, the major media have discovered that collectively, independent presses now control a significant share of the marketplace. In the fall of 1983, the R.R. Bowker Company (the former Xerox subsidiary that publishes *Library Journal* and *Publishers Weekly*) launched *Small Press*, an informative and tasteful bimonthly sold to the trade as well as to independent presses. In the fall of 1980, *The New Yorker* serialized Thomas Whiteside's disturbing book on commercial publishing and distribution, *The Blockbuster Complex*,[7] and the July 25, 1983 issue of *Newsweek* did a splendid article on four of the "giants" of independent publishing.[8]

Elementary and secondary school teachers have become increasingly sophisticated about the independent press through AIE residencies. Many writers have a knowledgeable approach to printing which aids the design and production of the writing "sampler," a residency requirement. Just as small presses have grown more knowledgeable about production, employing offset or letterpress in place of ditto or mimeo, school samplers have gotten away from crammed dittos reeking of alcohol, turning to computer typeset, photo offset books produced at the county vocational high school or at the local quick printer. Some schools with computers are now producing the entire sampler in-house.

The idea of the well-done book seems to be returning. Mass-market paperback publishers have virtually trashed the idea of the book, using lurid covers and text stock reminiscent of French toilet paper. However, many small publishers regard the book as an art object and some "fine" printers produce beautiful letterpress editions.[9] A new species of "artists' books" has also recently come into being.

Teachers are becoming more discriminating book buyers. Many book stores, especially the chains, will not stock small press titles, but will order them individually. Some stores participate in STOP (Single Title Order Plan) which facilitates individual orders. In addition, several distributors publish catalogs which are a great help in sorting through what otherwise appears to be a maze. Several review publications also help locate small press books of interest. (See bibliography.)

III. Some Conclusions

While there are no quantitative studies to prove that writing residencies have created a market for serious literature, the connection is undeniable. In the mid-1970s, Len Randolph, while still at the Endowment, attributed the growth of college/university creative writing programs to poetry residencies in elementary and secondary schools. I'm sure that despite the other contributing social factors, Randolph was correct, for the other social factors were also contributing to the interest in AIE programs.

In my own residency experience I have seen adults return to poetry as if to a forgotten memory, and children engage in it as a perfectly natural activity. I regularly witness audiences responding to poetry performances attached to symphonies and gallery openings. Individuals come away from the readings saying, "I never thought I would like poetry" and "I always thought poetry was too complicated to enjoy."

The literary revival offers surprising experiences. In the small river town of Marietta, Ohio, audiences of 150 to over 200 people *pay* to see readings by Gerald Stern, William Stafford and Gregory Orr on the Becky Thatcher Showboat.[10] The audiences include high school students, retired business people, government officials and ships' captains. Marietta isn't alone, for an increasing number of writers are finding audiences in communities apart from campuses.

AIE residencies have been creating audiences which in turn have aided the growth of alternative publishing and the preservation of serious writing. This is, in fact, a great oversimplification, for the literary revival itself is vast and diverse, encompassing every imaginable racial and ethnic group and every geographic area. It is a pluralistic phenomenon of such complex proportions that it could not be well-represented by a money-minded group of entrepreneurs located between Wall Street and Madison Avenue, who would prefer to ignore its existence. It is well-represented by the heterogeneous scattering of serious craftspeople comprising what poet James Bertolino has called a "literary biosphere" rather than a triangular hierarchy with power and influence at the apex.

The literary audience also continues to increase because of the imaginative and innovative use of public performance and collaborations of writers with artists in other genres. AIE programs, in fact, have helped reestablish the origins of literature as an oral art form. In addition to the writing, much of the classroom work in a residency is done aloud, but it all leads back to the written word, the book.

Just this morning I received a letter with a commemorative stamp titled "A Nation of Readers." Although the image of Abraham Lincoln reading to his son didn't seem to me to be representative of our time, I think we are once again becoming a people who care about the book. I recall one residency of mine where a high school sophomore not regarded as having any intellectual potential by his English teacher, was sparked by my residency into taking an avid interest in studying history. Almost every residency has at least one such success story. Books are being rediscovered as lasting instruments of pleasure and learning.

Contrary to the prophecies of some computer manufacturers, many of our contemporary writers will continue to be read (in book form) in the 21st century. As I see it, as our economy declines, our values will continue to shift from the material to the spiritual. As hardware, software and the cost of transportation continue to increase, we will take more active pleasure in reading and community forms of entertainment (involving the arts) rather than the high-tech pleasures of passive consumers.

Notes

[1] Koch's earliest experiments are described in *Wishes, Lies and Dreams* and *Rose, Where Did You Get That Red?* The books are published in paperback by Vintage and are widely available.

[2] The best single source of books is an organization that runs its own residency program and publishes and distributes books on the subject: Teachers & Writers, Inc., 5 Union Square West, New York, NY 10003. Write for a free catalog.

[3] *CODA, Poets & Writers Newsletter*, Vol. 6, No. 3, Feb./March 1979, New York, NY, p. 23.

[4] Remarks by Peter Davison, *The Publication of Poetry & Fiction, A Conference*, Library of Congress, Washington, DC, 1977, p. 6.

[5] Both the *International Directory* and the *Small Press Record* are published by Dustbooks, P.O. Box 100, Paradise, CA 95969.

[6] Len Fulton, *Tribal Energy*, a flyer advertising the *Whole COSMEP Catalog*, Dustbooks, *op. cit.*

[7] Published in 1981 by Wesleyan University Press.

[8] Three of the four are giants because they are heavily capitalized by millionaires. The four are at the apex in an economy of scale. The existence of hundreds of small publishers not interested in financial success in big terms is ignored by the article.

[9] I think of such presses as The Bieler Press in St. Paul, Adastra Press in Easthampton, MA, Salt-Works Press in Grenada, MS and the new Bloody Twin Press in Stout, OH.

[10] The charm of the showboat is not the reason for the draw, for the largest crowd came to the William Stafford reading at the Lafayette Hotel while the Becky Thatcher was in drydock for repairs.

Bibliography

Several state agencies publish annual or occasional anthologies from their AIE programs. The books are excellent sources of ideas. Many anthologies are free, some are available at the cost of production. North Carolina, Pennsylvania, Montana and California have all published interesting books.

An excellent source of reviews of literary titles from all presses is *The American Book Review*, P.O. Box 188, New York, NY 10003. It is a bimonthly tabloid. Other, more regional yet high quality tabloids are *The Boston Review*, *The Threepenny Review* (San Francisco) and *The Bloomsbury Review* (Denver).

I highly recommend ordering free catalogs from the following distributors:

Small Press Distribution
1784 Shattuck Avenue
Berkeley, CA 94709

Thurber Country
Thurber House
77 Jefferson Avenue
Columbus, OH 43215

Writers & Books
740 University Avenue
Rochester, NY 15607

Robert Fox has been on the staff of the Ohio Arts Council since 1977. A widely published fiction writer and poet, he is the author of *Destiny News* (December Press), a collection of short fiction and a novel, *The Second American Revolution* (Latitudes Press), forthcoming. He is also editor and publisher of Carpenter Press.

Innocence & Inertia & Other Dangers in Poetry in the Schools

/Ron Padgett

In January 1969, when Kenneth Koch invited me to teach poetry writing to elementary school children, the idea was new, the way Kenneth did it, anyway. But I didn't want to teach poetry to anyone. I just wanted to be a poet. I was 26, writing a lot, living by hook and crook, so why should I get a "job"?

Finally talked into sitting in on Kenneth's classes, I saw that he taught like a poet, fresh and unpredictable. His classroom discoveries came in on waves of pleasure and excitement. The kids loved him—a great cheer arose when he walked into the classroom. I thought to myself, "This is actually great, but . . . ulp, can I follow it?"

A few weeks later, he went on sabbatical and I took over his classes. The first day, afraid that the kids wouldn't accept me, I aped him shamelessly. I even borrowed his tone of voice and sense of irony. It worked! They liked me! They wrote poems! They were good poems! I went home! I wrote a diary account! I showed it to my wife! I told her every minuscule thing that had happened! We had dinner! A check would arrive! I was exhausted.

With more experience, I shifted from being Kenneth's understudy to being more "myself." The kids accepted the transition. I finished the school year, working with four classes per day, once a week. For this I was paid $50 per week, which covered artistic preparation, scheduling, classroom time and writing classroom diaries. My diary accounts tended to be lengthy, detailed and personal—I usually spent an hour or two on each one, writing it as soon as I got home and mailing it the next day to Teachers & Writers Collaborative (T&W), the sponsoring organization. I also kept the kids' poems and sent them to T&W, where they were mimeographed and mailed back to me for distribution at the school.

Some months went by before I even spoke with anyone at the T&W office. It never occurred to me to ask what T&W was, or even if it was OK that I now worked for them! I blithely steamed ahead in the classroom. Finally, attending a T&W meeting, I had little sense of the people as a group, which suited me fine: I had no interest in being part of any circle other than that of my immediate friends.

I was, though, starting to like the work. I enjoyed thinking up new poetry ideas and trying them out, both in the classroom and at home. I didn't have any elevated notions of reforming public education or "saving the kids," I just liked writing poetry with them. Gradually, though, I was being drawn out of the privacy I felt in being a poet. In my neighborhood, where the school was located, kids and their parents began to recognize me on the street, and when new acquaintances asked me what I did, I now answered that I was a poet.

A year or so later, I started to realize that my being in the school could have other consequences, larger or at least more general than that of getting the kids to write poetry. I started thinking about education and how it fit in with the way people behaved and thought (or didn't). It dawned on me that there were implications to teaching poetry in the classroom, whether I wanted to think about them or not, and that working with a group such as T&W could mean more than getting a check from them.

For one thing, T&W was having more than local impact. State arts councils, many of them new, were beginning to send poets into the schools, poets who looked to T&W publications for ideas and advice. Many of these poets made discoveries of their own, but T&W was the mother lode for teaching poetry in the schools. If you came up with something useful at T&W, chances were that it would be used all over the country. There was also at T&W a competitive comraderie that was stimulating for its members both as writers and as teachers of writing.

From 1969 to 1977, then, I taught poetry writing to children, their teachers and other adults, in New York City with T&W and in seven states with various Poets in the Schools (PITS) programs. The T&W residencies were for longer periods (I was in one school for five years, 30 days per year); the PITS residencies tended to be short, usually five or 10 days. After a few years, the PITS work grew tiresome because it called for too much salesmanship and left little room for experimentation. If a school spends its entire annual artistic budget for a poet to come in for a week, that poet is expected to produce results, not fool around with some weird, new idea that might flop. The PITS poet is highly accountable to the school and the state arts council, which is accountable to the state legislature, which is accountable to the electorate whose very children attend the school. So the poet, whose future residencies are always at stake, tends to stick with "successful" poetry writing procedures. This results in a dulling repetitiveness not unlike the traveling PITS poet's common experience of waking up in yet another motel but not knowing in what town or even what state. In short, if you're presentable, capable and durable enough, you will last for a while in the PITS program, but if your idea of poetry involves risk, you will eventually find it depressing to go into another classroom without the freedom to experiment. PITS programs have various kinds of burnout built in, but this one is particularly frustrating.

The early days of T&W were wide open. The group had been founded and furthered by writers of bold character, such as Herbert Kohl, Muriel Rukeyser, Grace Paley, Kenneth Koch, Clarence Major and Phillip Lopate, and the sense of possibilities was enormous, occasionally intoxicating, at times, wonderfully "unrealistic." The Literature Program of the National Endowment for the Arts (NEA), one of T&W's major funders at that time, encouraged artistic experimentation in the classroom. Many of T&W's host schools received the poet's services for free, and were quite happy to offer themselves as artistic laboratories.

After eight years, though, I had worked with every genre, every age group and every class size, and I came to the conclusion, no doubt premature, that I had tried everything I could try in a public school setting. There seemed to be no place for me to go, no way for me to build on what I had done.

T&W changed, too, and in many ways for the better. Its administration became more sophisticated in dealing with the public schools, funders and other arts organizations. It developed its own publications department. It expanded its classroom program while other idealistic groups of the 1960s were falling by the side. It developed a national reputation among teachers of writing. It continued to show real concern for its writers by treating them as writers, not as hirelings, and it provided unemployment benefits. But even T&W, an exemplary organization, has never been able to solve the burnout problem.

In this respect I have been lucky. I took a leave from T&W to work for two years with the South Carolina State Arts Commission in a special Writer in the Community program, and for several years after that, I directed the St. Mark's Poetry Project in New York. Then I returned to T&W to direct its publications program. After years of teaching writing, this last position has been a natural step. It has given me a way to extend my work in the classroom and to develop professionally, as an editor and publisher, that is, as a person who is still learning to write. It also offers freedom for experimentation. Such positions are few, and other poets who have burned out of teaching have not been so lucky in finding relevant work. All over the country, good poets become good poetry teachers only to find themselves forced out by burnout and into some disconnected way to earn a living.

Just as young poets new to teaching do not foresee the burnout that comes from repetitiveness, the organizations that hire them tend to become satisfied with successful methods and to grow set in their ways, too shortsighted to adjust to changing social, educational and political conditions. Personal innocence and organizational inertia are major internal threats to the vitality and independence of teaching poetry in the schools.

Such a situation has continued because of an absence of unity and leadership at a higher level. There is no national organization for poets teaching writing in the schools (T&W comes closest), there is little or no communication among all the state arts councils' writing programs and there has never been a single national meeting of poets from these programs. As to forming an overview of what poetry in the schools has been or might be, the NEA's Artists in Education program, which funds the state arts councils for their PITS programs, says it does not even have such basic statistics as how many poets have worked in state PITS programs over the years. We are sadly in disarray and it leaves us open to attack from the outside, an attack that has been long in coming.

The external threats take several forms. The most obvious is the current administration, whose policy regarding funding for the arts is blatantly destructive. The administration initially proposed a huge budget cut for the NEA, urging the "private sector" (corporations and foundations) to make up the difference. At the same time, the administration moved toward massive cuts in social programs. The private sector, suddenly faced with new and larger funding requests from all sides, had to feed the hungry and help cure the sick before providing us with art. And most of the corporate and foundation money left for the arts goes, as usual, to the more glamorous performing arts. To top it all off, the administration has now proposed eliminating corporate and foundation tax deductions for *all* their contributions. It's hard to understand how the private sector is supposed to support the arts if much of its incentive—tax breaks—is removed. With both state arts councils and the private sector running on empty, and with literature programs always a low priority in arts funding, you can imagine the result.

Another threat, unfortunately, sometimes turns out to be classroom teachers. I worked in many schools that had teachers who were known locally for their own poetry; they're usually the creative writing teacher or faculty advisor for the school literary magazine. Most of these teachers welcomed me warmly, but others lurked in the back of the room, territorial and tight-lipped. This adversary position can be described in more general terms as art education versus art in education. In teaching visual arts, the battle lines even have a history dating back to the founding of the NEA when federal funds for art instruction were moved from the U.S. Office of Education to the NEA. The National Art Education Association and other organizations took up the cudgel against artists usurping art teachers' roles, not to mention their jobs. There has never been a resolution of the problem, which, although centered in the visual arts, holds true for all the artistic disciplines. In the teaching of writing the conflict sometimes surfaces in the form of essay teacher versus poet.

Educators are gaining more and more control over how poetry writing is taught in the schools. Recently the New York Legislature allocated a considerable sum of money for an Arts in Education Initiative, with the funds to be managed by the New York State Council on the Arts. Rather than portioning out funds to the various Council divisions whose panelists are artists, the powers that be have created an entirely new division, with panels to consist of artists *and* educators. In this way, poetry in the schools is being shifted out of the literature division and into the hands of education officials. Not only are most school officials unlikely to be able to judge poetry, but they bring with them the bureaucratic frame of mind that is totally alien to its creation. I hope my forebodings about this new and well-intended funding prove unnecessary, but I don't think they will.

It's not that creative writers are always such great supporters of teaching poetry writing to children, either. Many writers have never understood the value of children as creators of poetry; they seem to think of childhood as an inferior form of adulthood, less worthy of the exaltation of poetry. And as arts funding grows tighter and tighter, more and more of these writers are saying, "Forget programs for children and poetry. Let's just have fellowships for individual, adult writers." In other words, to "real" writers, such as they are.

Another dubious development is *Beyond Creating: The Place for Art in America's Schools*, a report issued recently by the Getty Foundation. Getty hired the Rand Corporation to do a study on how to improve art instruction in the schools. The conclusion was that children should receive instruction in art history and aesthetics, as well as "art production." This idea has nothing fundamentally disagreeable about it. What is disagreeable is the tone of *Beyond Creating*: It looks and reads like an annual report to stockholders, full of the corporate-institutional diction that urges us to "effectively implement discipline-based art education programs" subject to "academic rigor," programs to teach children how to understand artists' "ideas." As if the purpose of art were to communicate ideas! I'm reminded of what the painter Fairfield Porter wrote: "Whenever I make a somewhat different painting someone is likely to ask, 'Is that a new direction?' They want to know what you are planning next. But I think this question arises from the misconception that what is interesting in painting are the ideas it expresses. Painters are concerned with things. The most prominent things in the painter's experience are right in front of him, like the paint on the canvas. It is better if he does not achieve a plan, and that the painting eludes him, with a life of its own . . . arbitrary and individual."

It's not surprising that those allied with the captains of industry should see drawing and painting and sculpture as "art production." It is disheartening, though, to think of the deadening effect such attitudes could have on the teaching of art. Like the educators who require lesson plans, monitor programs, conduct evaluations and submit reports, the ultimate message of the Getty report is that the wildness of art must be controlled, made to conform to middle and upper middle class standards of respectability.

Art, including the writing of poetry, must not be forced into the subservient role of being mainly the expression of any particular social group's idea of acceptability, particularly that of a non-artistic group. If poets who work in the schools and arts administrators who facilitate that work do not begin to defend their territory, I'm afraid that is just what will happen.

Is it inevitable that poetry teachers burn out, that the fresh discoveries of teaching poetry writing be systematized into staleness? I don't think so.

So, what's to be done? At the very least there should be a national meeting of poets and arts administrators of poetry in the schools. We need to assess our work and plan for its future. We might, for example, come up with ways to place poets in teachers' colleges, so teachers can be reached earlier in their careers. I don't know of a single teachers' college that has a poet on its faculty. It would be a logical and healthy role for the experienced poet. This is just one idea among what I assume would be many to result from a national meeting.

We should also be sure that such ideas would be heard by people in a position to make a difference. A set of resolutions signed by 50 poets would make little impression, but the same resolutions, endorsed by 50 state arts councils, would get the attention of legislators, local arts councils, school officials and teaching poets all over the country.

If something is to be done, now's the time. When NEA Chairman Frank Hodsoll says he's going to put greater emphasis on the arts in education, and when a state arts council as large as NYSCA announces an arts in education initiative, it means changes are coming. Poets should have their say before it's too late.

References

Beyond Creating: The Place for Art in America's Schools (Getty Center for Education in the Arts, Los Angeles, 1985).

Fairfield Porter (Hirschl & Adler Modern, New York, 1985).

Ron Padgett's books of poetry include *Great Balls of Fire, Toujours l'amour, Tulsa Kid, Triangles in the Afternoon* and *How to Be a Woodpecker*. He is director of publications at Teachers & Writers Collaborative in New York.

Photo © 1985 by Chris Felver

THE WORLD
IS
FLIPPIED
AND
DAMZLED ABOUT

An Anthology: 1982–1985

Barbara Angell
2851 Edgehill
Cleveland Heights, Ohio 44118
216/371-0441

Barbara began as a visual artist and illustrator and started writing poetry after her two-year-old son put stripes on a painting of a leopard. Her poems have been widely published in literary magazines and anthologies, and a collection of her work, *Games & Puzzles*, was published by Cleveland State University in 1978. She has been a member of a women's performing poetry troupe and the literature advisory panel of the Ohio Arts Council, and is currently giving readings as well as running the Coventry Library poetry series. Barbara has had wide experience in a variety of elementary and high schools. Currently, she is writing poetry, painting and working on a long prose piece.

Looking at a Portrait
While Wearing Bluejeans and Sneakers

of a woman with careless hair
curled over her ears,
long amber beads
and a fur.
You can smell her perfume,
its deep musk heavy with longing
or some old knowledge:
Russia, someone deposed,
snow blowing over a long field,
an ancient city by a river.

Shell polish on her nails,
brocade, thick aromatic coffee,
dark red wine,
she has escaped some country
with jewels sewn in her dress.

She poses in her fur,
eyelids smoky with shadow,
fragrant with jasmine, patchouli,
flowers from forgotten meadows.

I want to be that woman
with silk legs, a pearl button
on the strap of her shoe
and a purse with a crystal snap.
I want to be perfect, ready, unknown,
waiting for someone in a cafe,
waiting for me.

Scenes of Bluffton/*Debbie Augsburger*

Every fall, I see seniors
writing their names on the streets
in colors of red, white, yellow and blue.
Every fall, I see new seniors
painting over the old.

Ode to a Forgotten Teacher/*Brigette Herr*

You hear music, a piano is playing.
There are birds outside,
a silence inside you.
You see music on a page.
You look out and see the sun shining brightly,
flowers blooming.
You smell the grass through an open window,
you feel a breeze.
You want to go out,
but you must stay inside. Music engulfs you,
loud, then soft, chords, runs, phrases played freely.
You stop playing the piano; silence.
You are finished.

Hotwheels/*Tom Winklejohn*

I remember
there they were,
all in a row,
sleek, silver and shiny,
move to the speed of light,
so fast and small,
you just couldn't see them.
Sharp black rubber
and sleek chassis,
Now they sit, all alone,
not touched in years,
Where have all the good times gone?

/*Janet Plaugher*

As the horse
walked across the road, I
heard his shoes clicking on the road,
I saw his
mane and tail
blowing with the wind.

Springtime/*Merri Cooper*

As I
stand here
doing dishes,
I realize
that plants
all around
me are
sprouting,
blossoming,
growing.

/*Kelly Stover*

A journey through town,
The smell of gas,
A breeze swishing across my face,
A beep-beep, beep-beep
And a boy with his mother.

The smell of an apple sucker,
Gears shifting in a Coke truck,
The heat beating down on my arms
And a lonely wasp on a fire hydrant.

The aroma of fresh baked bread,
Dogs barking, yipping and yapping,
Stones under my feet, stumbling,
And a man repairing a roof.
This is my town of Bluffton.

/David Deitman

I remember
running after the animal beauty
the angelic form of grace and
I remember
catching it
and the disappointment of knowing
that nothing is perfect
no matter
how beautiful.

/Krissie Kowalewski

I feel like patterned frost
crinkling over windows
like crisp cool air whipping through the sky
I feel everyone is a snowflake
each one different from the other
I feel like fine wine bubbling from the bottle
but other times when I'm alone
I feel like frozen ice

But then again
the sun does come
and that feeling melts away

/Nino Frostino

There he sits
trying to figure
out his algebra
homework.
The room is
getting darker and
darker as he
sweats and sweats.
He scratches his
head and thinks
and thinks.

/Tonya Thornsberry

We sit together
    sharing thoughts
The wind blows quietly
            while the sun
                sets.

/Judy Chang

He stares
and looks up
to see

he sees
the blue sky
covered with clouds
and a sun

dreams
about
his future

Autobiographies of Famous People

Michelangelo/*Alisa Arenas*

Here I lie in the heavens of
the Sistine Chapel, my brush
moving ever so carefully as I
paint a stitch of lace on the
Virgin Mary's veil.
The paint drips on my face
as tears from heaven.
The pain in my back grows
more intense with every stroke
of the brush.
I stop my work for a moment
and look across the ceiling.
To my left is beautiful, bright
color. To my right is a vast,
empty whiteness, waiting for a
brush of the rainbow to touch it.
Below, the Pope bangs on the door
wanting to observe my work.
The door is locked, and it will
stay that way, for this is my world
and my world alone.
He surrenders to my army of silence.
A feel of victory rushes through
my body, and for a moment
the pain and strain are gone.
But then a drop of paint falls to
my face. My world reminds me
of my work.
I must continue.

Isaac Newton/*Mike Naylor*

As I sit down by my orchard
My parents work below on our farm,
The late summer breeze blows the pages
of my notebooks,
The yellow rays brighten up my work,
A strong breeze blows through the trees
overhead, dropping an apple to my side.
What caused it? A bird, a worm, or some-
thing else?

I look around,
I see other things fall, like leaves and rain.
Now I know the answer. The force that holds
the moon in orbit is the same that
makes the apples fall.

/*Joe Cleveland*

Here I am
standing by the old pine tree
watching my father wash
his old grey Volkswagen.
The sun is going down
and he throws two fishing poles
into the car, and we
head for our favorite spot
along the river.
I wish things never changed.

Columbian High School,
Tiffin

Beautiful Boxer/*Ronda Whitmer*

Sweat dripping
jab jab
from his hair
punch
making it
jab
cling
jab punch
to his face
jab jab
muscles in
punch jab
his legs are
jab
pumped to
punch punch
enormous
jab jab
size
jab punch
that look
punch jab
in his
jab
eye that
punch punch
wants to
jab punch
win so
punch
bad he can
punch jab
taste it

747/*Keith Halcomb*

An airplane
overhead
It is small
It looks like
a model
It can hardly
be heard
It leaves behind
a trail of
white dust
which gradually
fades away.

/*Lisa Mertes*

Staring straight ahead
stonelike and unmoving.
Yes, he still breathes,
a heartbeat exists.
Ears do not hear
the outside world.
Muscles disobey.
For nothing
can tempt
brother
from
the TV

Earl Butler
R.R. 1, Box 162C
Otway, Ohio 45657

Earl attended the University of Hawaii and received a bachelor's degree in English from Wright State University. He has worked as a reporter for the *Dayton Journal Herald*, a print shop artist, and as a field and mill hand. He was writing instructor and chairman of liberal arts at the School of the Dayton Art Institute until its demise in 1975. Two limited edition collections of his poetry have been published and a folding broadsheet collection is forthcoming. His work has appeared in *Live Writers, Maelstrom* and *Spitball*, and is forthcoming in *Pig Iron* and the *Spitball Anniversary Anthology*.

beech fork

the indian hen feeds in dead sassafras
drums across the grouse-thump spring

trillium   lady slippers   wild flag
abandoned easter flowers   gone short
ragged   a stand of lilies   deer path

cardinal flowers streak the summer
branch in crimson   orange orange leaps
of butterfly weed   purple fire ironweed
above a field of black-eyed susan claiming

forgotten pastures

sycamore bottom   shagbark squirrel tree
chestnuts still suckering still drying off

whiteoak   dry rattle of leaves   beech
silver clouds of beech
winter ghosts on the hill   in open
woods   shivering.

Dirty Man/*Kim McKnight, Grade 6*

Dirty man walks down street
in torn clothes and a bag in his
hand with clothes falling out behind.

Autumn/*Kari Waymire, Grade 6*

How good fresh hay smells
When it is carried from fields
as it gets pitch dark

How brisk the fall night
When amber colored leaves fall
While owls coo softly.

Butterfly/*Rachel Reveal, Grade 5*

The small butterfly
flies around the giant tree
then floats out of sight

Snowy Night/*Tony Artis, Grade 6*

One snowy night
we were driving on the highway
The snow covered the road.

Then came a snow plow
uncovered the road good
and then we went on.

When we went up the road
there was a very bad wreck
glass was on the road.

Night/*Tyson Frysinger, Grade 6*

Full moon glows brightly
Stars dot the endless night sky
Moon shines like grapefruit.

Animals asleep
Moonlight reflects off vast pond
Night air smells like pine.

Tall grass waves in wind
Tall pine trees stand straight
and strong
Stars look like snowflakes.

Haiku/*Don Briggs, Grade 6*

Gray ugly dumb sneakers
are walking on the hot road
the rain cools them off

My Poem About Coon Hunting/*Jason Lambert, Grade 8*

With the moon high above watching me
my dogs at my side
I set out for the woods.
There the woods stand like a thicket.
I turned my dogs loose
they scramble around
with their noses to the ground.
One lets out a yelp
the other comes to help.
Their ball mouths echo through the woods
Their long yelps turned to chops
they're treed.
I shined the tree to see a large coon
I shot out the coon.
The fight is over
and we have won.
Home we head
with a coon on my back
and my dogs at my side.

Racoon/*Christy Sharrett, Grade 6*

The fall wind chilly and cool
Blows through the trees and leaves
While I was sitting on my stool
I spot a racoon.

Fall wind chilly and cool
trees around are full
with yellow, red, orange leaves
a racoon walks to the creek.

My Mysterious Nightmare/*Scott Smith, Grade 8*

Flying on the fire
with my feet burning
flames to my head
scared and frightened
of the nightmare that
was upon me with
the air pockets pulling
me in and screaming
help me that was
the last breath I
took with the flames
turning red hot as
I was seeing my
body leave in the
fire as the body exploded
and the fire sprung
everywhere I watched
from above.

/Melissa Hartley, Grade 4

I feel so funny without a poem
in my mind. I need some help.

I feel like I should give a big yelp
but I just keep it inside.

When my friends come around I open my eyes wide
but when they go,
I wish that I could cry.

Roosevelt Elementary School, Portsmouth

/Scott Bailey, Grade 5

I walk down Second Street
On the coldest night in many years,
Watching the moon sail behind the misty clouds,
Pulling my cap over my cold ears.

I'm shivering as I turn the corner to the next street.
I light a cigar as I pull up my boots
And warm my wet feet.

I move on to the next street and see my house
Not far away and as I look up at the sun
Peeping through the clouds, I know
It's almost day.

Cold Morning/*Christina Charles, Grade 4*

Outside this morning
Our flowers covered with frost.
The yellow daffodil is now white
and the tiny purple crocuses
not quite so bright.
I know they will live on
Through the March snow.

/Leslie Irwin, Grade 5

I dream about a black
stallion, so sharp and quick
and so gentle to people around him.

I will get on him one day
and ride far away from life.
I know it.
And go to a land where
you can ride into the sunset.

And fly away into a dream land
far away where people have
fantasies all their lives and fall
into the real world and wake from wonderous dreams.

/Ricky Hickman, Grade 5

The little boat is sailing
on the blue water
and it comes back home.

Little Boys in White/*Lisa Weidner*

Little boys dressed in white
    march to a sergeant's threatening shouts
All the work, what is it for?
Grown up too fast
    pushed into a world
        of high technology
They fight to save their country
Dreams killed by a lack of ambition

Strong bodies rigid
    with the never ending tension
You have to cut it now
    or you'll never make it
Some hopes fulfilled
    others broken
The mental anguish is more
    than some can bear
    they seek solace in escaping forever
Without thinking
    the little boys in white
        march to a constant drum.

Atlantic/*Jill Snyder*

White foaming ocean
gritty sand entwined with sea
upward seagulls wail

Science Project/*Jim Hauenstein*

Tomato sauce in saturation,
Pepperoni bisected with elation,
Heated dough in plane so thin,
Spices mortared fine within.
A mass of cheese fused o'er the rest,
This is the project I like best.

Photo by Robert S. Wagner, Jr.

Hale Chatfield
13560 Old State Road
Huntsburg, Ohio 44046
216/632-5672

Hale is a professor of English and poet in residence at Hiram College where he founded the *Hiram Poetry Review*. He is the author of six volumes of poetry and one volume of short fiction. In addition, he has been the recipient of creative writing fellowships from the National Endowment for the Arts and the Ohio Arts Council. With NBC-TV, he and his colleague John Shaw taped a two-week educational series on poetry. He is an expert on the use of computers in teaching poetry, and in October 1985, he chaired a panel on that subject in Denver at the annual conference of the Association for Computing Machinery.

Boeing 737

I am not sure I understand
how energy is absorbent: the setting sun
draws this aircraft (art of air),
yet its light seems to push at my eyes.
I dream of electric tangerines.
Below in Ohio the snowy quilted fields
darken and do not call.
They are as still as tintypes,
and older. Where is home?
There have been millions of years.
I try to remember. The fallen sun pulls.
Mediate between earth and sky, this great lonely metal kite
floats like a life. I could live here.

(Reprinted by permission of the editors of *Hiram Poetry Review*.)

The Magic Barn

/Jerry, Grade 2

A magic cow can talk
A magic hen can dance.
A magic pig can fly.
A magic hen can play the drums.

/Racheal, Grade 2

All the animals can talk.
The hens lay eggs with blue
egg and red yolk. The cow
eats the eggs that the hen lays.

/Lewis, Grade 2

A hen jumps on the
magic cow the cow turns
the hen into a toad now
the toad is magic the
toad turns the duck
into a fox that's
how the animals change.

He's (She's) Not So Bad

/Chris, Grade 5

He's not so bad
He made his brother swallow a onion
He cut a frog in half
He put a bird in the blender
He's not so bad
He stuck tar on the toilet seat
He put grape juice in the dryer
He put gum in his sister's chair
He's not so bad.

/Taryn, Grade 6

She uses foul language to her preacher.
She gives her teacher a dirty diaper for Christmas
She makes her little sister eat hot peppers
with no water.
On hot days she makes her sister walk on cement
with no shoes.
She makes her brother chew aluminum foil.
She washes her sister's hair with glue.
She crushes fleas in her mother's orange juice.
She hangs the dog from the Christmas lights.
She's not so bad.

The Kangaroo Jumped Over the Fence with Ease
/Betsy Beans, Grade 6

THE animal is a creamy color of brown, he is a
KANGAROO. He has beautiful grace. Yesterday he easily
JUMPED over the fence. His bounce almost reached
the beautiful sky
OVER our heads. He looked carefully, surveying
the green land,
THE beautiful Australian countryside. He was leaving the
FENCE behind. For miles and miles he hopped very freely
WITH his head enjoying the moist breeze, taking
it all in with
EASE. Kangaroo, never remember your life before this time.

Feisty Kittens Roust in the Cool Summer Breeze
/Kyla Green, Grade 6

FEISTY little kittens play in the sun.
KITTENS run about nipping everyone.
ROUST as kittens will, fighting happily.
IN yowls one cries, bitten by a bee!
COOL waves pass, as if it were chasing a mouse.
SUMMER light beams onto the kitten's face.
BREEZE blows against her, and she's on the chase!

The Hideous Man Lifted a Thousand Pounds
/David Sternfeld, Grade 6

The announcer announced that the hideous man
chalked his weird hands.
"Man!"
The announcer said he had lifted ninety-nine
kilograms.
A photographer took thirteen thousand
pictures.
The Blade burned four pounds of pictures
at four o'clock.

The Things from Zerox Are Here
/Jenny Espersan, Grade 6

The things sing and dance and play, the
Things bite peoples heads off, the things
From Zerox will spit grapes on you
Zerox is a mean place, the things
Are crawling all over the ground.
Here they eat your toes and your nose.

Wise Elementary,
Streetsboro

Pantoums

/Karen Maskol, Grade 6

1 Homework
2 is very, very boring
3 so watch tv while doing it
4 or listen to a radio

2 is very, very boring
5 you can ignore it
4 or listen to a radio
6 it makes you sick

5 you can ignore it
7 let your dog eat it
6 it makes you sick
8 so throw it away

7 let your dog eat it
3 so watch tv while doing it
8 so throw it away
1 Homework

/Connie Boros, Grade 6

1 Drip
2 went the water
3 down the pipe
4 it was spring, drip

2 went the water
5 onto the cement
4 it was spring, drip
6 and everything was melting

5 onto the cement
7 because it was spring
6 and everything was melting
8 in the sun

7 because it was spring
3 down the pipe
8 in the sun
1 Drip

/Bobby Webb, Grade 6

1 I ate a cat for dinner
2 it was bad to eat a cat
3 but it go with shrimp
4 but I got sick from eating a cat

2 It was bad to eat a cat
5 when I got to the eyes I threw up
4 but I got sick from eating a cat
6 my dad came home he seen me eat a cat

5 when I got to the eyes I threw up
7 when I got to the liver it taste good
6 my dad came home he seen me eat a cat
8 at the end of eat a cat I got sick

7 when I got to the liver it taste good
3 but it go with shrimp
8 at the end of eat a cat I got sick
1 I ate a cat for dinner

/Gary Adkins, Grade 6

1 That hurts
2 said the little boy
3 I don't care said the man
4 why?

2 said the little boy
5 very sadly
4 why?
6 because I feel very bad.

5 very sadly
7 the boy said
6 because I feel very bad
8 I don't care

7 the boy said
3 I don't care said the man
8 I don't care
1 That hurts

Terry Hermsen
95 K Illinois Avenue
Westerville, Ohio 43081
614/891-2446

Originally from Michigan, Terry received a bachelor's degree from Wittenberg University. A bicyclist, he published *36 Spokes: The Bicycle Poems* in 1985 with Bottom Dog Press of Huron, Ohio. He has also published poems in such magazines as *Kansas Quarterly, Descant, South Dakota Review, Cincinnati Poetry Review* and *Pig Iron.* In the fall of 1982, Terry was poet in residence for the Springfield Arts Council, working with senior citizens, inmates and a women's group. He organized and narrated 10 radio programs about contemporary poetry in 1982 and 1983, produced and broadcast by WYSO in Yellow Springs.

–after working with my daughter on the violin

And silence: how is it like learning to move
another hand, waiting in the fingers, sparred
and tendoned, but trained in a different time?
A pact not to explain all at once. The hours
fight measure, and the ease with which words come,
dull taste of tar after repeated talking.

and no closer to cure, leaves, matted,
to break in the waterfall. The crucible
slow to boil down to its color. Patience
is all, teaching one finger its angle to hang
on the lip of a string, the eyes to follow an arm
up and down, up and down, up, up, and down.

My Dad/*Tiffany Eder, Grade 5*

As my dad leaves for work,
he's very loving, yet on the job very brutal.
Up a ladder he climbs, into a pit he digs,
thinking of what people are thinking as they
pass. He comes home
tired and sore, takes a shower and goes to sleep.
I think of him now,
still working, getting hurt, falling, and tearing
clothes, I feel proud
to have him as a father.

Back in Time

Terrors of War/*Pat Failor*

East Germany, 1941
The War was still all around me, there
Was a gunshot. I found myself dreaming.
Dreaming these same words over and over.
Like you see yourself in the TV
watching yourself watch TV
over and over
watching ourselves in Berlin.
The next day our troops
moved out to Berlin.
I found the TV
and I was inside
watching myself in Berlin

Talking to the Psychiatrist/*Craig Cabal, Grade 8*

When I went to work this morning, I saw a woman being robbed. I could of saved her or come to her rescue, but I didn't. I don't know why . . . I didn't assist her . . . I just don't know why . . . maybe I do. Maybe!! Maybe I had no business in stopping that lady from being robbed . . . I-I-I-felt that I was from another world and that I was only supposed to observe things—and I was not permitted to interfere with anything. I felt that I'm on a long curious voyage—a voyage to this world but—but I am of this world. I don't know—Maybe I'm crazy again——

Housemarks

Note: These poems and designs are in the ancient tradition of "housemarks"—symbols that families put above their doors and on their goods as a kind of brand or family seal.

/Drew Vonderahe, Grade 4

My sign is a crooked arrow.
Or a pyramid with a tunnel
at the bottom. Sometimes
I pretend I'm a Dead
King, but I'm not, and
I escape through the tunnel.

/Bob Attenweiler, Grade 4

My sign looks like a church
　　of the future without any past.
A boy with a nose like a lollypop.
Sometimes I feel I have no hope
when I step inside.
I go into the future
　not past.
I feel I am being swept away.

Beware the Jabberwock

Arunning Raway/*Liese Millikin, Grade 5*

The dumble fays and drampen bugs all occupy themselves,
While me and the fudwas play in the sun.
And the cooperdops and the riddledoos sing in the grass,
But the world is flippied and damzled about.

I flip down on the crench and the doon is down,
But I haven't gone home.
Dother and Mad come out to lind me,
And I ralk faway to the stream.
Mad has guven ip,
But I reep kunning.

Somewhere, outhere, that's a place for ye and mou,
But I don't wunderstand I don't even care,
'Cause someone's gonna come lookin',
Someone's gonna see,
Thaf wite rere I a'standin',
I'm stayin' here forever.

Coming Home

/Joy Bickimer

Mansfield, I'm back!
But where are you?
I can see you, but you don't move! I see someone
In a house. I knock on the door. But they don't
answer.
Mansfield you're like a frozen glass of pop. I can
see you but can't drink you.
Half of my life I lived here, and now I come back
and you're gone in the strangest way.

/Anonymous, Grade 6

Warren
Warren, you are like a bowling ball
rushing through mercury.
You are like a fishing pole ready to break
into many pieces
each piece going its own way.

Project Women
Writing Workshops
Springfield

/Colleen Robinson

My father flares
at the thought of shattered
glass on the carpet. It is
a mind waster.
He flares
at scattered minds wandering
across courtyards and deserts.
Tip-toe past the gates
they are closed forever.

My father is
ashamed of climbing fences and
falling into nowhere
There must always be a some-
where at the ending.
He is afraid of beginnings
I watch this man sink into
darkness while searching for
a steady stream of light that never
shines.

/Ruth Ann Riser

Sometimes I am a marble
Rolling almost to the edge
Catching myself before I do
For then I will be lost
Smooth, clear
Hurl me hard enough
I'll come bouncing back
Or maybe break in two
All the colors spilling

/Debra Dickerhoof

You are a poem of unwritten thought.
Blank page of contradiction,
words I've never spoken.
Imprinted on my mind's eye.
Present in your silence as
wind before storm.
Laughing,
while I, foot in mouth,
speak words, not yours,
and play the game of mockery–
ours.

/Jackie

I am
walking through the woods
I am afraid
So I stop for a moment
I see different kinds of things
The moon
The shining stars
Everywhere I go
It follows me behind
It seems so dark and solid
After all,
I think: the stillness
of the dark was
the shadow
I left behind

/Joe

I am a man
without a soul
I am a dream
without a picture
I am the sun
without its glow
I am alive
but yet I'm dead
I am a book
but cannot be read
I am a bird
that cannot sing
I am a forest
without trees
I am a flower
without its scent
I am a fire
but without a flame
I am a line
but have no end

/Vickie Feichtner

I sit and look at a sight that's
  not all there.
It's as if someone is trying to
  erase part of my memory.

The walls are there
but that is about all.
The ceilings have fallen where I
  once stood.

At the Abandoned Train Station/*Mike McCarthy*

The tracks are silent as the shade blankets me.
I look upon the ravages of age,
vines enstrangle,
choking the life out.
A truck rolls by and I, as it's passing by,
take but a moment's notice at the changes
of the endless vortex of time.

Cheerleading/*Tammy Moore*

I started to jump
As if jumping to the stars.
And as I came back down,
The sky was roaring
And cheering along with me,
And the roaring sky.
Moving upward toward the stars.

Swirl

/Brian Siesel

The day pulls long and hard like an old car
Pull the day old car and long hard-like
Hard like the day the old car pulls
The long car pulls hard like old days
Pull the day pull the car the day is hard
Long and hard like the day the car pulls
I feel the hard long pull of the day
The day feels my long pull like an old car

|Debbie Richards

My grandmother
                made thirty drastic
meals a day and wore
clothes that belonged to
her grandmother.

My grandmother
                spent the days
talking about her childhood,
and never worried about mine.

My grandmother
                loved her garden
but pulled the flowers and
left the weeds grow.

My grandmother
                recognized the
good in people—when there
wasn't much to look for.

Snatches

Note: A type of plagiarism, these poems resulted from lines jotted down after listening to poems by other students in the class. The lines, quickly chosen and coming from different authors, make poems by themselves. This was a new discovery for all of us.

/John Hines

As if someone has erased part of my memory
It's different sizes and shapes
I feel the bumps in the road
The chirping of the birds
Confusion greater than the greatest maze
Drifting

/Missy Ramey

A cloud hangs low as dark falls fast.
Nothing can take away the happiness I feel.
Being smothered by a great force.

Diane Kendig
328 Howard Street
Findlay, Ohio 48540
419/422-8313

Diane, who has taught every grade from kindergarten through graduate classes, presently teaches at Findlay College. She holds a bachelor's degree in Spanish and English from Otterbein College and a master's degree in English from Cleveland State University. The past year, she has been active in teaching writing to teachers and leading a creative writing workshop at the Lima prison. Her poetry and prose have been published in many magazines, anthologies and non-print media, and a collection of her poems, *A Tunnel of Flute Song*, was published in 1980. Forthcoming is a book of Nicaraguan poetry she translated.

On Dinosaurs and Poetry

Look, if I ask for your first memory
and you give me your parents' version,
whose poem is that? And if you describe dinosaurs,
neck and tail, skin so thick it could be tree bark,
if you copy the words "powerful" and "extinct,"
whose poem is that?

There are thousands of monsters in the past,
roaming, lost without you.
Your job is to find the one that's yours.
Don't tell me what others say it is like.
Start with the first thing you remember.
Now, back before that, to your grandparents.

Now, back before that, before any people:
Say you are a dinosaur–what do your neck and tail
feel like? And your skin? And how does it feel
being the largest thing in the world,
to be dying of that size?

Kindergarten Collaborations: Poems on Animals

Colts and Foals
/Mrs. Foltz's Class

First they eat milk, then
hay, oats, grass. They walk wiggly.
They move carefully.

Their coat is like fur.
They're little as us, little
as deer. We like them.

This Is a Cow and Bull Poem
/Mrs. Bethel's Class

They eat grass. They are brown
brown, white, black. Bulls are fathers.
Cows are mothers. They

say moo. They don't smell
that good. Calves are born wet. Some
give milk, some give meat.

First Grade
Creation Poems

Potato/*Matt Shook*

God put dirt in a brown paper bag. He put it in hot water and he cooked that. Cut it and ate it.

Principals/*Elizabeth Fye*

He took clouds and swooshed them all up. He put some nice sense in them. He used magic colors, and painted the clouds so it looked like a principal.

Second Grade
Acrostics

Winter/*Diane Sparks*

Dawn comes upon us slow
Icicles hang from the roof
Ants start to hide away
Noses sneeze and sneeze
Evergreen turns white.

Summer/*Donald Jewell*

Days are long in the summer,
Owls hoot in the night
Next day we go swimming.

Song of Ourselves
/Mrs. Clifford's Second Grade

We are hummingbirds
    and our class is a high nest.
We are bees because we work hard.
We are rockers
    and we like to rock

We are talkers for fun.

Third Grade
Humpback Whale Songs

A Whale/*Brad Stinnett*

Once upon a time,
I rode on a boat and all of a sudden
I heard a squeak,
I saw a black velvet suit,
It was a whale.

Lone Whale Talk/*Mindy Hall*

When you talk
Your sound is so very high,
You squeak and shriek,
Your moan sounds like crying,
Like you're saying *help me*.
Your blowhole sounds like a fountain.

Three Whales/*Steve Trompower*

I think I sound like a
haunted house,
I think I sound like a
broken record
I think I sound like a
bad violin.

Third Grade
Odes

Ode to the Duck/*Jason Stadtlander*

Oh little butterball,
Your rubbers are so orange.
Your eyes are so blue.
You feel so warm.
You look so cute.
Praise to you, duck.
I don't know what I would do without you.

Ode to Baseball/*Mike Schmidt*

Baseball, baseball,
I love thee,
I like to play
your game,
I love your
players,
I like to grip
your bats,
I like to throw
your baseballs,
I love to feel
the leather in your glove.

Ode to a Book/*Janice Crilly*

Oh book, with your many word-filled pages,
Your pictures are so colorful.
Your chapters are so exciting.
You give me something fun to do when
there's nothing happening.
Oh, book, life would be very boring without you.

Kangaroo/*Jeff Baker*

Oh you lazy animal
even though you can jump far.
You are shaped like a candy bar.
You smell awful.
You feel so furry and warm
You should live on a farm.
Oh, you lazy animal, you.

Ode to the Bell/*Rodney Thompson*

Oh bell, hurry up
Go ring, ring, ring
I like your sound
And you look like a party hat
You feel like a steel plate,
Oh, bell, hurry up.

Poems with Spanish words

The Fiesta/*Glen Glace*

Uno dos tres
off goes the fireworks
the fiesta begins
down by the rio,
little insects singing
un bello canto.

The Storm/*Lisa Listke*

The lluvia fell hard on the roof,
The thunder boomed and banged.
The lightning crashed to the suelo
And then the tumulto calmed down.

Haikus

Horses/*Jennifer Bobich*

Their tails flash against
the wind, their manes flap against
their face, their eyes glaze.

The Ant Sees Grass/*Brett Ulrich*

The grass is big, it's
over my head, it's as straight
as a line, and strong!

Fourth Grade

Poems based on John Haines' "If the Owl Calls Again . . ."

If the Dog Calls Again/*Jeff Rapp*

at night
from back in the woods
and it's not too hot

I'll wait until stars
come out
then I'll run to
meet him

when we meet we'll talk awhile
we'll talk about
our lives

then we'll run and play
we'll play by chasing cats
up a tree

but when the fun's over
we'll go back to
sleep

If a Flower Came to My Door
/Colleen Belcher

at noon
from the ocean far
and it is very hot
I will sit for the sun to rise
and take a smell on to noon.
I wouldn't talk very much,
just listen to what she said
and say hello there and then
we would close up at night
and open in the morning
as the world wakes, too.

If I Met a Buffalo/*Colleen Belcher*

at the beach
I would probably run across the sea
And he'd chase after me
then when all is quiet, I would
fall on my knees and cry
Please do not eat me, please!
And he would say, I will
not eat you
You are too sweet
and too nice. I
want to
ask you if you know
where Billy is.
I want to eat *him*.

Questions My Brother Asked Me,
Answers I Never Gave Him/*Wendy Remark*

1. Do monsters come out at night?
Yes, but they first hide under the refrigerator.

2. Do flowers bloom money?
No, but they give money to the bees when they take honey from the flowers.

3. Do poems talk to you?
Yes, when you want to hear the poem they'll read themselves to you.

4. Do sharpeners sharpen your pencils themselves?
Yes, when you're not allowed to sharpen your pencil . . . .

5. Are ghosts always white?
No, they are usually your favorite color.

6. Where does hair come from?
Your brain makes it and pokes holes in your head and sticks it through your head.

7. What does God look like?
He's purple and lives in California.

Joel Lipman
2720 Winsted
Toledo, Ohio 43606
419/473-0958 (H)
419/537-2983 (W)

Joel was born in Washington, D.C. and raised in Kenosha, Wisconsin. He attended the University of Wisconsin and the State University of New York at Buffalo and has degrees in English, law and humanities. He's taught widely in colleges and universities, grade schools and community arts organizations. He's received Ohio Arts Council Individual Artist Fellowships for both his writing and visual language work, and is a recipient of an OAC Governor's Award for the Arts in Ohio in 1985. He is the author of two poetry collections: *Chicago You Got a Wide Stance* (Piirto Press) and *Mercury Vapor Lamp* (Ocooch Mountain Press). Among his other awards and distinctions are a gorgeous wife and two beautiful children.

The Luna Moth

appears at night by quarter light
of moon. Luna leaves trees
along the low-lying meadow,
leaves grasses where land begins
a rise of hilltop, leaves eaves
where loft beams and barn roof meet.

A ghost of green iridescence
soundless from hickory grove to a cone
where light flows from the outdoor lamp
tonight beats the glass
of my window like a luminous bat.
What of the luna moth but that?

from *Mercury Vapor Lamp*

An Ode to My Bedroom/*Lisa R.*

Oh! bedroom you are always
clean,
When you could be as dirty as
a pig's pen.
Your walls have a nice shade
of pink on them.
I wonder if you ever get tired
of hearing our radio.
I wonder if you get mad when
I bring over a friend and they
lean on your wall.
Oh! bedroom you're like a
pot of gold that will keep shining.
You smell like fresh strawberries
When we spray
room fresher on you.

Ode to the Sun/*Carrie Closson*

Oh sun, oh sun, you keep me so
warm.
You're like a great big lightbulb
in the sky.
Even though I cannot smell you
sun, you give the flowers their
scent.
Even though I cannot hear you,
you make the birds sing.
Even though I cannot taste
you, you give the corn its taste.
And even though I cannot
touch you, your warmth
reaches down to me.
Oh sun, oh sun I love you so.

The Last Dinosaur/*Brent Racer/Grade 6*

I was on my way to a birthday party when I saw a enormous head stick out of a swamp. I thought someone was playing tricks on me. But before I knew it the enormous head led to a enormous body. It was longer than 4 semis plus trailers. It was so beautiful it looked better than Bo Derek in a little bathing suit. The only bad thing about it was its teeth. He had at least 100 sharp teeth and his biggest teeth could have been 4 feet long. I couldn't make out what kind it was. But if I know my dinosaurs I think it was a Apatasauras. I said to myself, "What is going on? Those dinosaurs were extinct almost 1 million years ago."

When it went back under I ran to the party I was going to and told everyone what I saw. Of course no one believed me. So I proved it to them. There really is a dinosaur in the swamp. Everyone was amazed by the outstanding animal that could live that long and not be seen by anyone. Once the story got out, our little city became more important than Washington, D.C. There were reports and television broadcasts about the dinosaur.

After we caught it we had to freeze it to make sure it wouldn't die on us. It was really scary when they brought it up from the swamp and put it in a cooler.

A month after that happening our town went back to normal.

Images/*Chris Dorn*

1. Too Slippery To Hold Onto
2. A Man As Skinny As A Broom Handle
3. Hitting Your Hand Instead of the Nail
4. As Brittle As A Centimeter Thick Sheet Of Ice
5. As Square As A Circle
6. A Dog Playing Tennis
7. A Black Flower
8. A Mouse Sinking in Quicksand
9. A Perfectly White Tablecloth With One Blotch Of Blood On It
10. A Book with No Words

I like
some sports
or I read books
I am a GOOD
CARD player I LOVE
a CHALLENGE playing
just about EVERY
game
call ME a
24 HOUR
CARD SHARK
or GAME HOG

Freddy Arrizola
2B

the MIRROR, got a LETTER. It was about a Mysterious crystal Stone.

Bobbi Mueller

HOW

SPECTACULAR

AND

fanciful

AND

luxurious

can

The

PRINCESS

be.

Julie Kurtz 6A

The Girl of Julie Cunningham

The Party/*Dave Delcoma*

Sweaty hands grasp
the cold bottles
submerged once in ice.
Their caps lying
on the table
the floor.
Ashtrays overrun with
butts
hazy smoke.
Half-intoxicated bodies
roam through
dim lights.
Speakers throw
high pitched sound
from every corner.
Everyone is happy.
Morning light peeks
into windows
sleepened bodies.
Bottles and cups
lay dead
some half alive.
Their poison floods
the carpet
bloodstreams.
It is over now.
The stream is tough
but the salmon
will make it.

Strasburgh High School
Tuscarawas County

Devon McNamara
Box 296
Philippi, West Virginia 26416
304/739-2471

Devon has degrees from New York University and the University of Illinois. In addition to teaching in a wide variety of settings in many states, she has worked for West Virginia Public Radio and written for *The Christian Science Monitor*. Her poems have appeared in such periodicals as *Dark Horse, The Hiram Poetry Review, The Laurel Review* and *Trellis.*

Opening Day

first time for everything
beginner's luck
opening to the right page
catching something immediately
native trout in its shimmer
wealth of the unsaid
catching something immediately
like that line drive
from Sandy Amoros
a Dodger
back in 55
at the Polo Grounds
really a foul
but don't get technical
it's my first game
Dad rises
to the occasion you might say
cupping his hands loose enough
to let it slam
into his stomach
knocking him clean out
long enough for me
to scramble under the boards
among the Cracker Jacks
and pick it up
my own sweet prize
Willie Mays signs it
Alvin Dark, Don Mueller, Ray Katt
Gail Davies, Hank Thompson
heroes in those old uniforms like pajamas
Giants in my earth
though I never got to another game
till after the Giants and Dodgers went west

more

Now it's on the tv
in a plastic doodad
to keep home runs in
sort of a mausoleum
no a pantheon   if you know what I mean
hard little sucker like that
smacks a man in the stomach
thirty years ago or so
to convince his daughter
she's lucky to be beginning, and
ought to be a poet about it

Excuses!/*Lee Sisson*

I can't write because–
I have someone on my mind.
My pencil is not sharp.
I am on drugs (I'm not).
I am on alcohol (I'm not).
There is too much noise,
Too much talking.
I am under the hood of a car.
I can't write with my left hand.
Not enough rock music.
I am in school.
I am in a class fire.
I am smoking.
Too much noise.
Too quiet.
The fan is blowing.
Teacher gets on your back.
It is greasy,
It is a heavy motor.
I like to work on cars.
It is a dirty job.
It fell off the blocks,
I got caught between the fenders.
The hood fell off on my head!

Going Public/*Theressa Mullen*

When fingernail polish was
  banned I had to paint behind
  my ears, and the bottom of
my feet.
When the teacher turned her
  head, I polished her shadow.
When the poet turned around I
  polished her tongue.
When I eat I always polish my
  bread.
I sleep at night dreaming of
  polishing the White House.
I wake up with a polish brush
  in my hand.
I get up early so I can catch
  Mom asleep and polish her
toenails a bright fluorescent
  orange.
When the ban was lifted, I
  bought 8 new colors and
  polished each of my finger-
  nails a different color,
  and polished the front of
  my ears and the top of my
  feet.
I polished the teacher's hand,
  and the poet's face.

Sometimes/*Jeff Warner*

Sometimes blood drips from the
clouds and hits my shadow
Sometimes I feel like a
tornado inside.
Sometimes I feel like I have
no eyes
Sometimes I feel like the 8
ball (left out)
Sometimes I feel like a ghost
Sometimes I feel like I've
been shot six times (once is
enough!)

Our Life/*Tara Danison*

My next door neighbor is
93. She had a yellow cat and
it fell in the vent and it
was very hot and the cat was
down there with no food and
no air.
After 2 or 3 days the cat dies
and she didn't know what to
do and I didn't know what to
do.
I have a yellow cat in every
one of my poems.

Laughter/*Beth Bailey*

When laughter was banned, I
   had to go elsewhere.
Where no one could hear or see me.
I had to hide behind the
   shadow of my hand, for
Fear if I were caught
the condemners would not understand.
In the darkness, giggling
   quietly, not to upset others
   as some have done.
Oh how I dream of letting
   laughter fill both my lungs,
   but
When they are not watching, I
   sneak a giggle here and there.
I hear it silently ring
   all through the air.
Giggles in the corners and cracks,
   hiding under the table
Never to be found. Oh yes,
   they search for them, I say
   not a word.
A laughter rings out behind
   their backs because I am so
   clever.
Echoing a distance, but still
   they do not hear.

Amber's First Day/*Sara Batata*

Amber's my sister
Her first day:
        she cries
        she weeps
        she screams
        she panics
A boy comes near
        picks on her
I go there
        I move him away
She's happy now
        I stay
        I go with her
She stays quiet
Sara goes with me
We all go home
Amber's first day at Nursery
    School—brave for all.

Everybody Wants You
/Brad Hughes

Everybody wants you
I feel left out.
Everybody needs you around
To survive, it seems.
I am less than 2% of the
U.S. recommended
daily allowance
as a friend.
She's so popular
I can't stand it.
No, not anymore.
The ground is flying
up toward my
suicide.

/Matt Quatman, Grade 2

Hello hose
Good-bye toes
Hello food
Good-bye candy
Hello God
Good-bye Devil
Hello wiggle
Good-bye tooth.

St. Charles School,
Findlay

Things That Have No Name
/Julie Wiltsie, Grade 7

The funny sound you hear
  when you yawn.
That feeling you get
  when you hear something when you're asleep.
The feeling you get
  when you get caught talking
  and the teacher yells at you.
The feeling you get when you wake up
  and can't make a fist.
The startled feeling you get
  when the bell rings
  and you aren't ready for class.
The feeling you get
  when you just finished reading a long book.
The feeling you get
  when your stomach groans.

St. Charles at Night
/Jennifer Baggs, Grade 6

Snowflakes punching at the U.S. flag,
at the school yard.
The steel desks sitting in the
dusty classroom.
Shooting stars are glistening
through the bitter cold night

When They Banned Time
/Jennifer Gallant, Grade 6

My watch stopped.
We stayed the same age.
Our hair wouldn't grow.
Our book would stay on the same page.
The snow was in mid-air.
When they lifted the ban on time . . .
My watch started and
The snow was falling.

/Mike Schaefer, Grade 6

I went to bed as a lemon
and I woke up as a tree.
I went to bed as a potato
and I woke up as the earth.
I went to bed as a tree
and I woke up as a worm.
I went to bed as a piece of paper
and I woke up as a pen.
I went to bed in my room
and woke up in the ocean.
I went to bed in my bed
and woke up in the mouth
of a whale.

Malaki
1907 Knowles
East Cleveland, Ohio 44112
216/681-6517

Malaki attended Fisk University where he received a bachelor's degree in economics in 1973. There he studied with writers Robert Hayden, Arna Bontemps and John O. Killens. Malaki coordinates arts programs for various school systems and arts institutions in the greater Cleveland community and is currently involved in making an instructional videotape of his classroom teaching techniques for libraries and educational institutions. He has read in colleges and universities from Texas to New York and has had a collection of his poetry, *tracks*, published by Konglomerati Press in 1979.

honey

honey was
dazzling dark eyes,
brand spankin' new dimes
spinning
on the edge of time,
a gingerbread jail
i was caught up in her smile,
her smell!
honey was
a glistening, golden
casual liquid jewel
prettied by a mother's care,
ribbons in her hair,
fresh
and flirting with my imagination.
my, how she enjoyed the chase
and me
gasping for breath
almost choking on my laughter
blinded by a blur
of black patent leather and
legs.
she could run so fast
her age would change
in chase.
i honestly didn't know/care
whether she was real or not
and until you
                    smiled
i'd forgotten
all about the taste of honey

Born Beneath the Stars/*Kirsten Sohn*

as I stand on the land
leaning against a fence,
I watch two horses
cantering in the moonlight
across a field.
the stars are bright,
it's a beautiful night
with the wind blowing
as if knowing
that a foal was to be born.
I watched the mares
by the light of the moon
as if I'm sure a foal is going to be born.
Blinka laid down then as if she knew
that her enemies were few.
and then, I saw her black body quiver
and as only the moon and I know
a beautiful foal, the color of snow,
was born under the stars' watchful eyes.

Your Little Corner/*Amy Houghtling*

Have you ever gone to
a corner of your own?
In your corner, have
you ever forgotten
who you were?
In your corner do you
pretend you are someone
else?
In your corner
all day long, do you day
dream?
In your corner
do you ever fall asleep?
In your corner
do you ever just think?
What do you do
in your corner?

The Khorogo

/Angel Koehl

An African Khorogo,
filled with many thoughts,
trying to talk, but not
knowing what to say.
Pictures—a man, fishing
for the flying fish painted
next to him.
A man, hunting for the birds
and wild animals
all 'round him.
Trying to survive in Africa
on an African Khorogo.

/Gina Wikas

The Khorogo spoke to me
as if it wanted to dance.
It sang and danced in
the moonlight.
It moved to the beat of
the pounding drums.
Slower then faster,
Faster than slower.
Moving in beautiful patterns,
Slowing down and then
stopping.

Bluegill Pond/*Tammy Rude*

As I sit in the shade
under the tree
the wind is blowing and I can feel a breeze.
I look at the pond,
the sunlight is shining on it
and the little breeze leaving little ripples
in the water.

Wading/*Cyndi Gaylor*

As we were wading, we
could have seen a salamander,
but we didn't.
We could have seen a crawdad,
but we didn't.
We could have kept our gym shoes
nice and clean and dry,
but we didn't.

**Morton Junior High School,
Vandalia**

Nick Muska
534 Nesslewood
Toledo, Ohio 43610
419/246-1249

Nick holds degrees in literature and English from Antioch College and the University of California, Santa Barbara. He has participated in poetry festivals and workshops in France, England and the Netherlands, as well as in this country. In 1979, as head artist/coordinator of the Arts Commission of Greater Toledo's Inmate Arts Program, he began teaching creative writing workshops to inmates at the county jail and prison farm, a program he continues with support from the Ohio Arts Council and the Toledo Poets Center. His first collection of poems, *ELM*, recounts his experience as an industrial warehouseman in Toledo. His work has appeared in such periodicals as the *Chicago Review, Wabash Review* and *Rockbottom*. In 1984, Bloody Twin Press produced a limited edition letterpress folio of his *Three Key West Sunsets*. He is the recipient of three OAC Individual Artist Fellowships, a 1983 Toledo Arts Award for Community Impact and a Governor's Award for the Arts in Ohio 1985.

Self-Portrait Before a Class of Sixth Graders

I wave my arms, big hands limp
counting the kids who've tried the poem
so they'll line up in front of the video.
I, too, mumble and stumble, and kimbalay—
that hitch in my walk, that finger at the side of my nose,
those too long teeth as I bite off "e-nun-ci-ate!"
Oh, I know my fried face well, but I seem almost deaf
as I cup my ear over and again to hear the voices,
the small voices aimed into their books, lost in desktops,
in other incomplete directions.
When I stress the importance of clear speech,
          of speaking to the back
of the room, I am a machine all agog—who would want to
          sound *that* way?
Makes my skin itch—and I do look itchy, but cannot scratch.
Finally, this poem, mumbled through no mask.
An uneasy sight. Have I taught? Do I teach?
Do I reach them? Enrich them? Get the child up
                    from his seat?
No. They will find voice. They will speak.

Old Orchard Elementary
Toledo, Ohio
March 12, 1985

Comparisons

Ed Is Like/*David N. McCusher*

I name you Super Smarty.
You look like a chattering chimp.
        (because of your mouth)
You are a Dandy Lion
You are greasy, fried chicken.
You taste like an Almond Joy.
        (because you're so nutty)
You are like a mostly sunny day.
        (you're a pretty good kid)
You are like a topaz.

/*Andrea Anita Ellison*

I call you snowball
You look like the rabbit Angora.
You are a yellow daffodil.
You are a baby kitten playing with yarn.
You taste like Strawberry Swirl ice cream.
You remind me of flowers.
You sound like a bird chirping.
You are a precious lock.
You remind me of 12 pm
You are California. So pretty.
You're a plum and peach.

Julia/*Chris McConnell*

I name you baby blue
You look like a baby white tiger cub
You are a pink carnation
You are a watchamacalit
You are like cherry cheese cake
You remind me of a summer
evening when the sun is setting
on the horizon.
You remind me of a cool crisp
spring day.
You sound like the leaves blowing
on the trees in spring.

Sound Poems

Barrel Drum/*Matt Weaver*

Noises banging in the night,
bam, bam, boom, boom, etc., etc.
Tribes of Indians chanting side
to side and dancing to the beat
of the Barrel Drum, aarooom,
aaroooom, the medicine man
driving out the evil spirits
far away from the tribe, fire
rising and noises are louder,
singing and dancing to the
sounds of the Barrel Drum,
bam, bam, boom, boom,
Groooooaroo!

Word Play on "Lactescence"
/Sabura Wilson

Lack essence
Black dresses
Ba jessies
My messes
My message
Die meo sage
I miss dave
Buy this cave
By this grave
Badis grade
Gladdus made
Glad as aid
Dad has ate
Dan is eight
Had estate
Had a date.

Making Stew/*Anonymous*

1. Add carrot
2. Spit at it
3. Let your dog play in it
4. Chant a magic spell
5. Add a hotdog
6. Chop it up
7. Add sour lemon
8. Leave it alone
9. Let the bees at it.

Lanaya in Yugoslavia/*DeAndra Moore, Grade 6*

Lanaya
    Who is in Yugoslavia swimming in
    a deep blue pool with fish, tiny gold fish
    which have no sense at all, running around
    wildly in the water, with different hormones
    inside of them, just like you and me.
        I think

Yugoslavia
    A place where people and animals go to
    mate in the water flowing down from
    the mountains. Tall, rough ended, deep dark
    blue mountains.

I'll go there one day
but first
I have to go look on the class map
To find out where I'm going.

Sixth Grade
Poems based on Mayan Glyphs

Getting a Bathtub/*Carol Riedel*

There it is, the faucet
O, I really like it
Even my dog likes it.
It even has a soap holder
and towel holder
and comes with a big towel
and a pretty knob to turn it.
Let's have a party in it
and wear bow ties.

/Matt Weaver

Backwards torch with a handle
A bucktooth Indian man with a cone head.
A dog dancing in an Indian tribe—all dressed up.
A Chinese woman dancing, also to music.
A cob of corn that's very wide, and has a hollow hole in it.
An Egyptian man in the desert looking through a telescope.
A planet with deformed rings on top of it.
A fat girl over in Africa walking home from school with
a backpack on.
A scarecrow with a snake as the pole.

Sick/*Carol Riedel*

I don't feel well
I'm really shaking
I'm getting bumps all over
I'm getting weak all over
My tonsils are swollen
My tongue is getting shorter
My nose—I can't feel it
My tail is curling up
O, my God, I fell apart!
I think I'm sick.

Fifth Grade
Translytics after Mayan Glyphs

Dig Godzilla/*Chad K.*

We can drink elephant wine
So we wrote "den."
Ryan enters near Dr. Jenny and she ends
her spine. An inn named zebra
uses a frog or a tarpon, eats a running
chipmunk. A pelican enters
a porcupine den. "Gluk" said the
porcupine. Larry walks in as
a slave. And he's wearing mittens.

Morning and Afternoon/*Anonymous*

The sun comes up you awaken
You milk the cow your wife yells at you.
You make your bed and take out your wrench
You fix the wagon wheel you sit on your couch
You see your couch on T.V. The sun is high
You make tracks in the mud you walk down the road
You get a phone call it was the realty
You left the phone off the hook so they don't call
again you listen to your radio.

No T.V./*Scott Noel*

(Translytic based on "No Te Veo"
by Pedro Salinas)

No T.V.. what a bad sight
Can you imagine no "Aqua Deserts."
No "Doomed Fragile Couple,"
No "Lady Lords Your Turn To Call Them"?
All insane
No "Michael Von Sir Llama"?
Please, no radio
Tell Mom now!
I can do nothing. Al will never
watch a "Verne" show again!
I try to imagine living with no T.V.
And get nowhere, a pity on me.
You guessed it: "Boston Hay Lover"
is on Channel 13.
Again no trivia games
Oh man, who did this?
All a dirty joke, huh?!
Fragile cord you are now alive.
This is the way to watch
    my soap Boperas.

Jane Somerville
608 Seventh Street
Marietta, Ohio 45750
614/373-7391 (H)
304/424-8000 (W)

Jane has degrees from Ohio University and Columbia University. She has taught literature and creative writing at Jersey City State College and Parkersburg Community College; has developed and directed writing workshops for older citizens in West Virginia nursing homes, libraries and senior residences; and has presented many workshops on the teaching of writing. Her poems, stories and critical articles have appeared in nearly 80 publications including *The American Book Review, The Greenfield Review, The Ohio Review* and *The American Poetry Review.* Jane reviews poetry for the *Cleveland Plain Dealer* and other publications; edits *Gambit*, a regional journal; and is founder of the Ohio Valley Literary Group, which presents readings on the Marietta showboat, Becky Thatcher.

Tonight

Stars slung up
like staves
above the garden
to keep us safe.
This is the night!
The hour beyond
relapse, the
apparition,
when the small birds
rattle in the bush, the grackles
roll their throats,
the monkeys stare,
the big faithful
elephants come
lifting their trunks.
It's a children's story.
We'll sit here
in the porch swing
kicking the floor,
playing our parts.
Gregg will sling
firecrackers out
the upstairs window
as a signal. Time
to begin. Now
in the barrel of night
we will pronounce
each word
carefully: bird star sky
flute wind
mother, night.

Family Poems

My Brother Robbie/*Jody B., Grade 5*

1. He is an angry little boy.
2. He is short and fat.
3. I remember one day we were in the car. And we were throwing around a hanky. He blew his nose on it and threw it at me.
4. He likes to bowl even though he is three.
5. One day we were at the bowling alley. He wanted to bowl and we let him. He did better than me.
6. I remember when he was born. Well, I lived in Georgia, but I got a picture of him in the mail. He was adorable.

Grandmother/*Donald Smith, Grade 4*

1. She loves me too much, I think.
2. We went to all the MacDonalds in Tampa, Fla.
3. She has taken me everywhere I want to go.
4. Once I ran away from home to see her.
5. I think she does too much for me.

My Mother/*Trina Thompson, Grade 5*

1. She cooks a good meal every day for our family.
2. She has pretty hair on her head. It is black.
3. She has brown eyes. Also very pretty teeth.
4. She's laid off from Ford Motor Company.
5. She worked at St. Rita's Hospital.
6. She likes roller skating.
7. She curls her hair every day.

Grandfather/*Cynthia, Grade 6*

1. He liked to go fishing on a hot day.
2. He liked to sit on the porch and watch the stars at night.
3. I remember when he got angry at me he would sit down and talk to me.
4. He liked to play the guitar.
5. He bought me a doll on my fourth birthday.
6. He had black and white hair.
7. He died on his 69th birthday.

Mom/*Tonya Mallory, Grade 6*

1. She is light-skinned like me.
2. She has lots of friends that like her a lot.
3. She goes outside in the summer and sits for an hour and comes in with a sunburn. And makes me rub Noxzema on her back.
4. She has short fingernails.
5. When she's nervous she always scratches her arm.
6. Her name is Bertha Mae Thurman.
7. She has red hair and a little black.
8. She would make you stand in the corner if you do something or talk back to her.
9. When she is angry with me she calls me Cheree. And I walk slow to see if she will forget what she called me for.

My Grandma Alexander
/Cindy George, Grade 5

1. She had 11 children.
2. She helped rear 26 other children.
3. She was gentle with kids.
4. She had black hair and blue eyes.
5. She loved flowers and plants.
6. She loved the outdoors and fresh air.
7. She worked on a farm all her life.
8. She was blind.

I Am a Lamp/*Andrea Miller, Grade 6*

I am a lamp; I'm fragile.
round, smooth, and becoming.
My head is cream-colored linen, and lacy.
My arm is black, but it can only work when
        I'm plugged in: it turns on
and makes me bright. My body
is ceramic, painted dark brown.
I sit on a young lady's desk.

I haven't shocked her yet
because she's very careful. But one time
my brain had a blowout
because she did all her homework on the desk.

Sometimes she takes me to a stand by her bed
and reads all night instead of sleeping.
But all in all, I'm happy that
I help her to be a genius!

Screwdriver/*Mike Cope, Grade 1*

I can unscrew a screw or
I could put out your eye.
I am red like the fire or
I could roll on your desk.
I can work, work, work.

I Am an Angry Rain Cloud
/Elizabeth Young, Grade 5

I am an angry rain cloud
dipped in mud.
When I get angry, I rattle
and shake and
pour rain down
from the sky. I'm squeezed
by giant invisible hands–
when I'm mad.

You wouldn't want to
see me when I'm mad
because I'm disgusting–
when I'm mad.

I can do damage
beyond your wildest dreams:
hurricanes, floods, and
tornados–
when I'm mad.

While poems from all participating schools could not be included, here is a list of all the schools that did have writing residencies during the years covered by this collection.

Poetry and Creative Writing Residencies
1982-1983

Apple Creek Elementary School, Apple Creek
Bluffton High School, Bluffton
Clay High School, Portsmouth
Cloverleaf Jr. High School, Seville
Donnell Jr. High School, Findlay
Donnelsville Elementary School, Donnelsville
Edison Elementary School, Lima
Emerson Elementary School, Lima
Faurot Elementary School, Lima
Gallia County Local Schools, Gallipolis
Gallipolis City School District, Gallipolis
Glenwood Jr. High School, Findlay
Indian Valley School, Enon
Irving Elementary School, Lima
Liberty Union-Thurston Elementary School, Baltimore
Maplewood Elementary School, Lima
Morton Jr. High School, Vandalia
New Carlisle-Bethel Local School, New Carlisle
Northmont City Schools, Englewood
Northwest Local Schools, Canal Fulton
Ottawa-Glandorf Local Schools, Ottawa
Park Layne Elementary School, New Carlisle
Roosevelt Elementary School, Lima
Roosevelt Elementary School, Portsmouth
St. Michael School, Findlay
Seaborn Elementary School, Mineral Ridge
Seville Elementary School, Seville

Shiloh School, Shiloh
Smith Jr. High School, Vandalia
Summit Elementary School, Cincinnati
Tiffin Arts Council, Tiffin
Tuscarawas County Brd. of Education, New Philadelphia
Westfield Elementary School, Westfield Center
Whittier Elementary School, Findlay
Whittier Elementary School, Lima

Poetry and Creative Writing Residencies 1983-1984

Bethel-Tate Arts Council, Bethel
Bluffton High School, Bluffton
Cardinal Local School District, Middlefield
Central Jr. High School, Findlay
Cloverleaf High School, Lodi
Cloverleaf Jr. High School, Seville
Greene County Board of Education, Xenia
Jacobs Elementary School, Findlay
Jenkins Elementary School, West Portsmouth
The Miami Valley School, Dayton
Miami View Elementary School, South Charleston
Mills Elementary School, Sandusky
Ottawa-Glandorf Local Schools, Ottawa
Park Layne Elementary School, New Carlisle
Project Woman, Springfield
Raymer School, Toledo
St. Michael School, Findlay
St. Peter's Elementary School, Mansfield
Springfield North High School, Springfield
Streetsboro Middle School, Streetsboro
Tiffin Arts Council, Tiffin
Tuscarawas County Brd. of Education, New Philadelphia
Western Reserve Academy, Hudson

Poetry and Creative Writing Residencies
1984-1985

Arcadia Elementary School, Arcadia
Bluffton High School, Bluffton
Buckeye Central High School, New Washington
Deveaux Junior High School, Toledo
Dorr Street Elementary School, Toledo
Jacobs Elementary School, Findlay
Lodi Elementary School, Lodi
Miller High School, Hemlock
Northwest Local School Dist., Canal Fulton
Old Orchard Elementary School, Toledo
Sanderson Elementary School, Lancaster
Shiloh School, Shiloh
St. Charles School, Lima
St. Peter's Elementary School, Mansfield
Stranahan Elementary School, Toledo
Sugarcreek Elementary School, Bellbrook
Westlake City Schools, Westlake
Wilson Vance Elem. School, Findlay
Wise Elementary, Streetsboro